Java 11 and 12 – New Features

Learn about Project Amber and the latest developments in the Java language and platform

Mala Gupta

BIRMINGHAM - MUMBAI

Java 11 and 12 – New Features

Commissioning Editor: Aaron Lazar
Acquisition Editor: Alok Dhuri
Content Development Editor: Rohit Singh
Technical Editor: Gaurav Gala
Copy Editor: Safis Editing
Project Coordinator: Vaidehi Sawant
Proofreader: Safis Editing
Indexer: Priyanka Dhadke
Graphics: Alishon Mendonsa
Production Coordinator: Deepika Naik

First published: March 2019

Production reference: 1220319

Published by Packt Publishing Ltd.
Livery Place
35 Livery Street
Birmingham
B3 2PB, UK.

ISBN 978-1-78913-327-1

www.packtpub.com

`mapt.io`

Mapt is an online digital library that gives you full access to over 5,000 books and videos, as well as industry leading tools to help you plan your personal development and advance your career. For more information, please visit our website.

Why subscribe?

- Spend less time learning and more time coding with practical eBooks and Videos from over 4,000 industry professionals

- Improve your learning with Skill Plans built especially for you

- Get a free eBook or video every month

- Mapt is fully searchable

- Copy and paste, print, and bookmark content

Packt.com

Did you know that Packt offers eBook versions of every book published, with PDF and ePub files available? You can upgrade to the eBook version at `www.packt.com` and as a print book customer, you are entitled to a discount on the eBook copy. Get in touch with us at `customercare@packtpub.com` for more details.

At `www.packt.com`, you can also read a collection of free technical articles, sign up for a range of free newsletters, and receive exclusive discounts and offers on Packt books and eBooks.

Contributors

About the author

Mala Gupta, a Java champion, works as a developer advocate for JetBrains. Founder at eJavaGuru, she has been actively supporting Java certification as a path to career advancement. Since 2006, she has been coaching students and professionals with a view to achieving success in these certifications.

A frequent speaker at industry conferences, her Java books with Manning Publications, USA, are top-rated for Oracle certification around the globe. She has over 18 years of experience in the software industry. Mala has also co-founded KaagZevar, a platform for nurturing creativity as an essential life skill. She co-leads the Delhi Java User Group. As the Director of Women Who Code Delhi, she also drives initiatives for diversity advocacy for Women in Technology.

About the reviewer

Marcus Biel works as the customer experience director for Red Hat. He is a well-known software craftsman, Java influencer, and Clean Code Evangelist. He is also a regular speaker at Java conferences all over the world, such as JBCN Conf Barcelona, JPoint Moscow, and JAX London. Furthermore, he has worked as a technical reviewer for renowned Java publications, including *Effective Java, Core Java SE 9 for the Impatient*, or *Java by Comparison*. Marcus has worked on various Java-related projects since 2001, mainly in the financial and telecommunications industries.

When taking a break from Java, he likes hiking in the Alps, as well as backpacking, dancing, and enjoying a good beer or wine. He lives with his wife and baby son.

Packt is searching for authors like you

If you're interested in becoming an author for Packt, please visit authors.packtpub.com and apply today. We have worked with thousands of developers and tech professionals, just like you, to help them share their insight with the global tech community. You can make a general application, apply for a specific hot topic that we are recruiting an author for, or submit your own idea.

Table of Contents

Preface

With Java moving forward at a great pace, programmers must be aware of the latest developments to make the best use of its newer features in their applications and libraries.

This book will take you through the developments in the Java language, right from Java 10, to Java 11, and Java 12. The book deep dives into the latest developments in the language. You'll learn how these features can help you advance your development with the language and make your applications leaner and faster.

You'll also discover features to configure your virtual machine to reduce startup time, so as to solve throughput and latency challenges in the future. With the help of this book, you will overcome the challenges involved in migrating to new versions of Java.

Who this book is for

If you're an executive or solutions architect responsible for technology selection or Java migration decisions, this Java book is for you. You'll also benefit from this book if you're a computer science enthusiast curious to learn about the latest, and upcoming, Java features. *Java 11 and 12 – New Features* will help you migrate your solutions from Java 8 or previous versions to the latest Java release.

What this book covers

Chapter 1, *Type Inference*, introduces type inference with local variables, which was introduced in Java 10. You will learn how to use the var keyword and also the challenges involved.

Chapter 2, *AppCDS*, covers **Application Class-Data Sharing** (**AppCDS**), which extends **Class-Data Sharing** (**CDS**). You will learn about both and see them in action.

Chapter 3, *Garbage Collector Optimizations*, discusses the various GCs and their interfaces for efficient implementation.

Chapter 4, *Miscellaneous Improvements in JDK 10*, covers the features and improvements in Java 10.

Chapter 5, *Local Variable Syntax for Lambda Parameters*, explains the local variable syntax for lambda parameters with an introduction to the usage of var with lambda parameters. This chapter also covers its syntax and usage, along with the challenges you may face.

Chapter 6, *Epsilon GC*, exploreshow Java 11 introduces Epsilon, which reduces the latency in garbage collection. This chapter explains why it is required and its design considerations.

Chapter 7, *The HTTP Client API*, talks about the HTTP Client API, which enables your Java code to request HTTP resources over a network.

Chapter 8, *ZGC*, explores a new GC called ZGC, which is scalable with low latency. You will learn about its features and work through examples.

Chapter 9, *Flight Recorder and Mission Control*, talks about the JFR profiler, which helps to record data, and the MC tool, which helps in the analysis of the collected data.

Chapter 10, *Miscellaneous Improvements in JDK 11*, covers the features and improvements in Java 11.

Chapter 11, *Switch Expressions*, covers switch expressions, which are a basic language construct enhanced in Java 12. You will learn how to use these to make your code more efficient.

Chapter 12, *Miscellaneous Improvements in JDK 12*, covers the features and improvements in Java 12.

Chapter 13, *Enhanced Enums in Project Amber*, shows how enums introduced type safety to constants. This chapter also covers how each enum constant can have its own distinct state and behavior.

Chapter 14, *Data Classes and Their Usage*, covers how the data classes in Project Amber are bringing about language changes to define data carrier classes.

Chapter 15, *Raw String Literals*, covers the challenges that developers face when storing various types of multiline text values as string values. Raw string literals address these concerns, also significantly improving the writability and readability of multiline string values.

Chapter 16, *Lambda Leftovers*, shows how the lambda leftovers project is improving the functional programming syntax and experience in Java.

Chapter 17, *Pattern Matching*, works through coding examples to help you understand how pattern matching can change how you write everyday code.

To get the most out of this book

Some prior Java knowledge will be beneficial and all the requisite instructions are added to the respective chapters.

Download the example code files

You can download the example code files for this book from your account at www.packtpub.com. If you purchased this book elsewhere, you can visit www.packtpub.com/support and register to have the files emailed directly to you.

You can download the code files by following these steps:

1. Log in or register at www.packtpub.com.
2. Select the **SUPPORT** tab.
3. Click on **Code Downloads & Errata**.
4. Enter the name of the book in the **Search** box and follow the onscreen instructions.

Once the file is downloaded, please make sure that you unzip or extract the folder using the latest version of:

* WinRAR/7-Zip for Windows
* Zipeg/iZip/UnRarX for Mac
* 7-Zip/PeaZip for Linux

The code bundle for the book is also hosted on GitHub at https://github.com/PacktPublishing/Java-11-and-12-New-Features. In case there's an update to the code, it will be updated on the existing GitHub repository.

We also have other code bundles from our rich catalog of books and videos available at https://github.com/PacktPublishing/. Check them out!

Download the color images

We also provide a PDF file that has color images of the screenshots/diagrams used in this book. You can download it here: https://www.packtpub.com/sites/default/files/downloads/9781789133271_ColorImages.pdf.

Conventions used

There are a number of text conventions used throughout this book.

`CodeInText`: Indicates code words in text, database table names, folder names, filenames, file extensions, pathnames, dummy URLs, user input, and Twitter handles. Here is an example: "The `PUT` request is used to create or update an entity on a server, using a URI."

A block of code is set as follows:

```
class GarmentFactory {
    void createShirts() {
        Shirt redShirtS = new Shirt(Size.SMALL, Color.red);
```

When we wish to draw your attention to a particular part of a code block, the relevant lines or items are set in bold:

```
abstract record JVMLanguage(String name, int year);
record Conference(String name, String venue, DateTime when);
```

Any command-line input or output is written as follows:

```
java -Xshare:dump
```

Bold: Indicates a new term, an important word, or words that you see on screen. For example, words in menus or dialog boxes appear in the text like this. Here is an example: "As you will notice, the **Lock Instances** option displays an exclamation mark right next to it."

 Warnings or important notes appear like this.

 Tips and tricks appear like this.

Get in touch

Feedback from our readers is always welcome.

General feedback: Email `feedback@packtpub.com` and mention the book title in the subject of your message. If you have questions about any aspect of this book, please email us at `questions@packtpub.com`.

Errata: Although we have taken every care to ensure the accuracy of our content, mistakes do happen. If you have found a mistake in this book, we would be grateful if you would report this to us. Please visit `www.packtpub.com/submit-errata`, selecting your book, clicking on the Errata Submission Form link, and entering the details.

Piracy: If you come across any illegal copies of our works in any form on the internet, we would be grateful if you would provide us with the location address or website name. Please contact us at `copyright@packtpub.com` with a link to the material.

If you are interested in becoming an author: If there is a topic that you have expertise in, and you are interested in either writing or contributing to a book, please visit `authors.packtpub.com`.

Reviews

Please leave a review. Once you have read and used this book, why not leave a review on the site that you purchased it from? Potential readers can then see and use your unbiased opinion to make purchase decisions, we at Packt can understand what you think about our products, and our authors can see your feedback on their book. Thank you!

For more information about Packt, please visit `packtpub.com`.

Section 1: JDK 10

This section will help you get started with type inferencing, which was one of the main features of Java 10. We will then learn about application class data sharing, which helps in selecting application classes in the shared archived files. Moving on, we will explore more about the GC interface and parallel full GC for G1. Lastly, we will cover the remaining additions or updates to Java 10, most of which are related to changes in the JDK or its implementation.

The following chapters will be covered in this section:

- Chapter 1, *Type Inference*
- Chapter 2, *AppCDS*
- Chapter 3, *Garbage Collector Optimizations*
- Chapter 4, *Miscellaneous Improvements in JDK 10*

1
Type Inference

The ability to use type inference with local variables (var) is one of the star features of Java 10. It reduces the verbosity of the language without compromising Java's dependable static binding and type safety. The compiler infers the type by using the information available in the code, and adds it to the bytecode that it generates.

Every new concept has its own set of benefits, limitations, and complexities. Using type inference with var is no exception. As you work through this chapter, using var will enthrall and frustrate you, but you will emerge triumphantly.

In this chapter, we'll cover the following topics:

- What is type inference?
- Type inference with var
- Dos and don'ts of working with var
- Type inference versus dynamic binding

What is type inference?

Imagine solving a riddle, such as the one shown in the following image, with multiple constraints in the form of hints. You resolve the constraints to derive the answer. You can compare type inference to generating constraints and then resolving them, in order to determine the data types in a programming language. Type inference is the capability of the compiler to determine the type of the data, by using the information that is already available in the code—literal values, method invocations, and their declarations. For a developer, type inference reduces verbosity, as indicated by the following diagram:

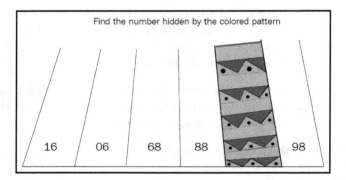

Find the number hidden by the colored pattern

For your reference, the answer to the preceding riddle is 87 (just turn the image upside down, and you'll find the numbers in a sequence).

Type inference is not new to Java. It has been taken to the next level with the introduction of `var` (with local variables) in Java 10.

Let's dive into the topic by looking at some examples of `var`.

Type inference with var

The following lines of code show how local variables (and all other variables) were defined prior to Java 10:

```
String name = "Java Everywhere";
LocalDateTime dateTime = new LocalDateTime.now();
```

Starting with Java 10, by using `var`, you can drop the mandatory explicit type in the declaration of local variables, as follows:

```
var name = "Java Everywhere";            // variable 'name' inferred as
                                         // String
var dateTime = new LocalDateTime.now();  // var 'dateTime' inferred as
                                         // LocalDateTime
```

Does it look like the preceding code doesn't offer a lot of benefits? Imagine you could take the following code:

```
HashMap<Integer, String> map = new HashMap<Integer, String>();
```

And replace it with this code, instead:

```
var map = new HashMap<Integer, String>();
```

By replacing `HashMap<Integer, String>` with `var`, the preceding line of code is much shorter.

When you move away from explicitly stating the data type of the variables, the compiler takes over to determine, or infer, the variable type. Type inference is the compiler's ability to evaluate the information that is already present in the code, like the literal values, operations, and method invocations or their declarations, to determine the variable type. It follows a set of rules to infer the variable type. As a developer, when you choose type inference with `var`, you should be aware of the compiler's inference algorithm, so that you don't get unexpected results.

With every new feature, you should adhere to a few rules and restrictions and try to follow the best practices to benefit from that feature. Let's start with the compulsory initialization of the variables that are defined using `var`.

 Type inference with `var` is not dynamic typing; Java is still a strong, static-typed language. The usage of `var` makes your code leaner; you can drop the type of the local variable from its definition.

Compulsory non-null initialization

A local variable defined with `var` must be initialized with its declaration, or the code won't compile. The compiler can't infer the type of an uninitialized variable or a variable that is assigned a `null` value. The following code won't compile:

```
var minAge;              // uninitialized variable
var age = null;          // variable assigned a null value
```

The following image illustrates what would happen if the uninitialized variable `age` went to seek entrance to the Mr. Java compiler place. The compiler won't let `age` in:

 Variable definition using `var` must always be accompanied by its initialization, or the code will fail to compile.

Local variables

The usage of `var` is limited to local variables. These variables are used to store intermediate values and have the shortest life span, as compared to the instance and static variables. The local variables are defined within a method, constructor, or initializer block (both instance and static). Within a method or initializer, they can be defined within constructs, such as `if..else` loops, `switch` statements, and the `try-with-resources` construct.

The following is an example of `Person` class, showing possible usage of `var` to define local variables in initializer blocks, methods (including constructors), loops, as a local variable within `switch` branches, or a `try with resources` statement:

```
public class Person {
    {
        var name = "Aqua Blue";            // instance initializer block
    }

    static {
        var anotherLocalVar = 19876;       // static initializer block
    }

    Person() {
        var ctr = 10;                      // constructor
        for (var loopCtr = 0; loopCtr < 10; ++loopCtr) {    // loop -
                                                            // for
            switch(loopCtr) {
                case 7 :{
                    var probability = ctr / loopCtr;       // switch
                    System.out.println(probability);
                    break;
                }
            }
        }
    }

    public String readFile() throws IOException {
        var filePath = "data.txt";
        // try with resources
        try (var reader = new BufferedReader(new FileReader(filePath))) {
            return reader.readLine();
        }
    }
}
```

As you can notice from the preceding code, a local variable can be declared using `var` at varied places in a class. Do you remember most of them? If not, let's make it simple for you.

Let's use an application to *find* all possible places where you could define local variables using `var` and mark it pictorially:

```
class Person {

    {
        ●                          // instance initializer block
    }
    static {                       // static initializer block
        ●
    }
    Person ( ) {                   // constructor
        ●
        if (....) {                // if construct
            ●
        }
    }
    void aMethod () {
        switch (..) {
            case .. : {
                ●                  // switch constructs
            }
        }
        ●                          // at beginning,
    }                              // middle or end
                                   // of a method
    for ( ● ) {                    // for - loop initialization
        ●                          // for loop body
    }                              // do, do - while loops
}
```

 This chapter includes a couple of code-check exercises for you to try. The exercises use the names of two hypothetical programmers—Pavni and Aarav.

Code check – part 1

One of our programmers, Aarav, refactored some code by his team member, Pavni. The code no longer provides `char` and the corresponding ASCII numbers of the values stored by the `char` array. Can you help Aarav? The following is the code to use:

```java
class Foo {
    public static void main(String args[]) {
        try {
            char[] name = new char[]{'S','t','r','i','n','g'};
            for (var c : name) {
                System.out.println(c + ":"   + (c + 1 - 1));
            }
```

```
        }
        catch (var e) {
            //code
        }
    }
}
```

The answer to the code check: The `var` type can't be used to specify the types of exceptions in the `catch` handler, `(var e)`.

Using var with primitive data types

Using `var` with primitive data types seems to be the simplest scenario, but appearances can be deceptive. Try to execute the following code:

```
var counter = 9_009_998_992_887;        // code doesn't compile
```

You might assume that an integer literal value (9_009_998_992_887, in this case) that doesn't fit into the range of primitive `int` types will be inferred to be a `long` type. However, this doesn't happen. Since the default type of an integer literal value is `int`, you'll have to append the preceding value with the suffix `L` or `l`, as follows:

```
var counter = 9_009_998_992_887L;        // code compiles
```

Similarly, for an `int` literal value to be inferred as a `char` type, you must use an explicit cast, as follows:

```
var aChar = (char)91;
```

What is the result when you divide 5 by 2? Did you think it's 2.5? This isn't how it (always) works in Java! When integer values are used as operands in the division, the result is not a decimal number, but an integer value. The fraction part is dropped, to get the result as an integer. Though this is normal, it might seem weird when you expect the compiler to infer the type of your variable. The following is an example of this:

```
// type of result inferred as int; 'result' stores 2
var divResult = 5/2;

// result of (5/2), that is 2 casted to a double; divResult stores 2.0
var divResult = (double)(5/ 2);

// operation of a double and int results in a double; divResult stores
// 2.5
var divResult = (double)5/ 2;
```

Though these cases aren't specifically related to the `var` type, the developer's assumption that the compiler will infer a specific type results in a mismatch. Here's a quick diagram to help you remember this:

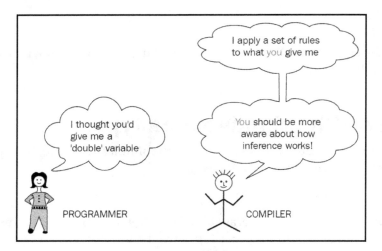

 The default type of integer literals is `int`, and the default type of floating point numbers is `double`. Assigning `100` to a variable defined with `var` will infer its type as `int`, not `byte` or `short`.

In arithmetic operation, if either of the operands is `char`, `byte`, `short`, or `int`, the result is at least promoted to `int`:

```
byte b1 = 10;
char c1 = 9;
var sum = b1 + c1;          // inferred type of sum is int
```

Similarly, for an arithmetic operation that includes at least one operand as a `long`, `float`, or `double` value, the result is promoted to the type `long`, `float`, or `double`, respectively:

```
byte cupsOfCoffee = 10;
long population = 10L;
float weight = 79.8f;
double distance = 198654.77;

var total1 = cupsOfCoffee + population;     // inferred type of total1
                                            // is long
var total2 = distance + population;         // inferred type of total2
                                            // is double
var total3 = weight + population;       // inferred type of total3 is
```

```
                    // float
```

 The rules of the implicit widening of primitive variables play an important role in understanding how the Java compiler infers variables with primitive values.

Type inference with derived classes

In JDK 9 and other previous versions, you could define a variable of the base class and assign an instance of its derived class to it. The members that you could access using the variable were limited to the ones that were defined in the base class. This is no longer the case with var, since the type of the variable is inferred by using the specific type of the instance that is assigned to it.

Imagine a class Child extends a class Parent. When you create a local variable and assign it an instance of the Child class, the type of the variable is inferred as Child. This looks simple. The following is an example:

```java
class Parent {
    void whistle() {
        System.out.println("Parent-Whistle");
    }
}
class Child extends Parent {
    void whistle() {
        System.out.println("Child-Whistle");
    }
    void stand() {
        System.out.println("Child-stand");
    }
}
class Test{
    public static void main(String[] args) {
        var obj = new Child();
        obj.whistle();
        obj.stand();      // type of obj inferred as Child
    }
}
```

What happens if you assign the value of the `obj` variable using a method that can return an instance of the `Child` class or `Parent` classes? Here's the modified code:

```java
class Parent {
    void whistle() {
        System.out.println("Parent-Whistle");
    }
}

class Child extends Parent {
    void whistle() {
        System.out.println("Child-Whistle");
    }
    void stand() {
        System.out.println("Child-stand");
    }
}

class Test{
    public static Parent getObject(String type) {
        if (type.equals("Parent"))
            return new Parent();
        else
            return new Child();
    }

    public static void main(String[] args) {
        var obj = getObject("Child");
        obj.whistle();
        obj.stand();                // This line doesn't compile
    }
}
```

In the preceding code, the type of the instance returned by the `getObject()` method can't be determined before the code execution. During compilation, the type of the `obj` variable is inferred as `Parent`, the return type of the `getObject()` method. Since the `Parent` class doesn't define `stand()`, the `main()` methods fail to compile.

 The types of variables defined using `var` are inferred at compile time. If the return type of a method is used to assign a variable that is defined using `var`, its inferred type is the return type of the method, not the type of the instance returned during runtime.

Type inference with interfaces

Let's extend the content of the preceding section to the use of interfaces. Imagine that the Child class implements a MarathonRunner interface, as follows:

```java
interface MarathonRunner{
    default void run() {
        System.out.println("I'm a marathon runner");
    }
}

class Child implements MarathonRunner {
    void whistle() {
        System.out.println("Child-Whistle");
    }
    void stand() {
        System.out.println("Child-stand");
    }
}
```

Let's define an obj local variable, assigning it an instance of the Child class:

```java
class Test{
    public static void main(String[] args) {
        var obj = new Child();              // inferred type of var obj
                                            // is Child
        obj.whistle();
        obj.stand();
        obj.run();
    }
}
```

If the same variable is initialized using a method whose return type is MarathonRunner, its inferred type is MarathonRunner (irrespective of the type of the instance returned by it):

```java
class Test{
    public static MarathonRunner getObject() {
        return new Child();
    }
    public static void main(String[] args) {
        var obj = getObject();      // inferred type of var obj is
                                    // MarathonRunner
        obj.whistle();
        obj.stand();
        obj.run();
    }
}
```

Using var with arrays

Using `var` doesn't imply just dropping the type of the local variable; what remains should enable the compiler to infer its type. Imagine a method that defines an array of the `char` type, as follows:

```
char name[] = {'S','t','r','i','n','g'};
```

You can't replace the data type name, that is, `char`, in the preceding code with `var` and define it using any of the following code samples:

```
var name[] = {'S','t','r','i','n','g'};
var[] name = {'S','t','r','i','n','g'};
var name = {'S','t','r','i','n','g'};
```

Here's one of the ways to include relevant information, so that the compiler can infer the type:

```
var name = new char[]{'S','t','r','i','n','g'};
```

It seems like the Java compiler is already struggling with this assumption from the programmers, as shown in the following image:

You can't just drop the data types in order to use `var`. What remains should enable the compiler to infer the type of the value being assigned.

Type inference with generics

Generics were introduced in Java to promote type safety. It enabled developers to specify their intentions of using classes, interfaces, and collection classes with fixed types or a range of types. Violations of these intentions were enforced with compilation errors, rather than runtime exceptions, raising the compliance bar.

For example, the following shows how you would define `ArrayList` to store `String` values (repeating `<String>` is optional, on the right-hand side of the assignment):

```
List<String> names = new ArrayList<>();
```

However, replacing `List<String>` with `var` will put the type safety of the generics at stake:

```
var names = new ArrayList<>();
names.add(1);
names.add("Mala");
names.add(10.9);
names.add(true);
```

The preceding code allows for the addition of multiple data types to `names`, which is not the intention. With generics, the preferred approach is to make relevant information available to the compiler, so that it can infer its type correctly:

```
var names = new ArrayList<String>();
```

> When using `var` with generics, ensure that you pass the relevant data types within the angular brackets on the right-hand side of the assignment, so that you don't lose type safety.

Now, it's time for our next code check.

Code check – part 2

One of our programmers, Pavni, tried using `var` with generics and collection classes, but her code doesn't seem to output the sorted collection of pens. Can you help? Check out the following code:

```
class Pen implements Comparable<Pen> {
    String name;
    double price;
    public Pen(String name, double price) {
```

```
        this.name = name;
        this.price = price;
    }
    public int compareTo(Pen pen) {
        return ((int)(this.price - pen.price));
    }
    public String toString() {
        return name;
    }
    public static void main(String   args[]) {
        var pen1 = new Pen("Lateral",   219.9);
        var pen2 = new Pen("Pinker",    19.9);
        var pen3 = new Pen("Simplie",   159.9);
        var penList = List.of(pen1, pen2,   pen3);
        Collections.sort(penList);
        for (var a : penList)
            System.out.println(a);
    }
}
```

The answer to the code check: The issue here is trying to modify the immutable collection by using `Collections.sort()`. This is to emphasize that not all issues are related to the use of `var`.

Passing inferred variables to a method

Though the use of `var` is limited to the declaration of local variables, these variables (both primitive and reference) can be passed to methods as values. The inferred types and the types expected by the methods must match, to allow the code to compile.

In the following example code, the `Child` class implements the `MarathonRunner` interface. The `start()` method in the `Marathon` class expects the `MarathonRunner` object (the instances of the class implementing this interface) as its method argument. The inferred type of the `aRunner` variable is `Child`. Since the `Child` class implements `MarathonRunner`, `aRunner` can be passed to the `start()` method, the inferred type of `aRunner` (`Child`) and the expected type of `start()` (`MarathonRunner`) match, allowing the code to compile.

The code is as follows:

```
interface MarathonRunner {
    default void run() {
        System.out.println("I'm a marathon runner");
    }
```

```
}
class Child implements MarathonRunner {
    void whistle() {
        System.out.println("Child-Whistle");
    }
    void stand() {
        System.out.println("Child-stand");
    }
}
class Marathon {
    public static void main(String[] args) {
        var aRunner = new Child();          // Inferred type is Child
        start(aRunner);                     // ok to pass it to method start
                                            // (param - MarathonRunner)
    }
    public static void start(MarathonRunner runner) {
        runner.run();
    }
}
```

 As long as the inferred type of a variable matches the type of the method parameter, it can be passed to it as an argument.

Reassigning values to inferred variables

As is applicable to all non-final variables, you can reassign value to inferred variables. Just ensure that the reassigned value matches its inferred type. In the following code, since the type of the age variable is inferred as int, you can't assign a decimal value of 10.9 to it. Similarly, since the type of the query variable is inferred as StringBuilder. The type of a variable is inferred just once, as follows:

```
var age = 9;        // type of variable age inferred as int
age = 10.9;         // can't assign 10.9 to variable of type int

var query = new StringBuilder("SELECT");        // Type of variable
                                            // query is StringBuilder
query = query.toString() + "FROM" + "TABLE";    // won't compile;
                                                // can't assign String
                                                // to variable query
```

The type of a local variable defined using `var` is inferred only once.

Explicit casting with inferred variables

Imagine that a co-programmer assigned 29 to an inferred local variable (let's say `age`), assuming that the compiler would infer the type of the variable `age` as `byte`:

```
var age = 29;          // inferred type of age is int
```

However, the compiler would infer the type of the variable `age` as `int`, since the default type of an integer literal value is `int`. To fix the preceding assumption, you can either use the explicit data type or override the compiler's default inference mechanism by using explicit casting, as follows:

```
byte age = 29;          // Option 1 - no type inference
var age = (byte)29;     // Option 2 - explicit casting
```

By using explicit casting type inference, you can override the compiler's default type inference mechanism. This might be required to fix the assumptions in the existing code.

Similarly, you can use explicit casting with other primitive data types, like `char` and `float`:

```
var letter = (char)97;      // inferred type of letter is char
var debit = (float)17.9;    // inferred type of debit is float
```

Without the explicit casting in the preceding examples, variables that are assigned integer literal values would be inferred as `int`, and decimal as `double`.

The following example shows explicit casting with reference variables:

```
class Automobile {}
class Car extends Automobile {
    void check() {}
}
class Test{
    public static void main(String[] args) {
        var obj = (Automobile)new Car();
        obj.check();       // Won't compile; type of obj is Automobile
```

```
    }
}
```

 Use explicit casting with type inference to fix any existing assumptions. I wouldn't recommend using explicit casting to initialize inferred variables; it defeats the purpose of using var.

Assigning null with explicit casting

Again, although it doesn't make sense to use explicit casting with null to assign it to a var type, it is a valid code, shown as follows:

```
var name = (String)null;          // Code compiles
```

Though the preceding line of code is correct syntax-wise, it is a bad coding practice. Avoid it!

Type inference in previous versions of Java

Although var takes inference to a new level in Java 10, the concept of type inference existed in Java's previous versions. Let's look at some examples of type inference in the previous versions of Java.

Type inference in Java 5

Generics introduced a type system to enable the developers to abstract over types. It restricted a class, interface, or method to working with instances of specified types, providing compile type safety. Generics were defined to add compile type safety to the Collections framework. Generics enable programs to detect certain bugs during compilation, so they can't creep into the runtime code.

Java used type inference for generic method type arguments in Java 5. Consider the following code:

```
List<Integer> myListOfIntegers = Collections.<Integer>emptyList(); // 1
```

Instead of the preceding code, you could use the following code:

```
List<Integer> myListOfIntegers = Collections.emptyList(); // 1
```

Type inference in Java 7

Java 7 introduced type inference for constructor arguments with generics. Consider the following line of code:

```
List<String> myThings = new ArrayList<String>();
```

In Java 7, the preceding line of code could be replaced with the following:

```
List<String> myThings = new ArrayList<>();
```

The preceding code shouldn't be confused with the following, which is trying to mix the generics with the raw types:

```
List<String> myThings = new ArrayList();
```

Java 7 also allowed type inference to invoke generic methods. For a generic method (say, `print()`) defined in a class (say, `MyClass`), the code would be as follows:

```
class MyClass<T> {
    public <X> void print(X x) {
          System.out.println(x.getClass());
    }
}
```

The preceding code can be called in either of the following ways (the third line of code uses type inference to infer the type of the argument passed to the `print()` method):

```
MyClass<String> myClass = new MyClass<>();
myClass.<Boolean>deliver(new Boolean("true"));
myClass.deliver(new Boolean("true"));
```

Type inference in Java 8

Java, version 8, introduced functional programming, with lambda functions. The lambda expression can infer the type of its formal parameters. Consider the following code:

```
Consumer<String> consumer = (String s) -> System.out.println(s);
```

Instead of the preceding code, you could type the following code:

```
Consumer<String> consumer = s -> System.out.print(s);
```

Challenges

The use of var doesn't come without its share of challenges, for both the developers of the Java language and its users. Let's start with the reasons why var has limited usage.

Limiting the scope of failed assumptions

As you know, the use of var types is limited to local variables in Java. They are not allowed in the public API, as method parameters or as the return type of methods. Some languages support type inference for all types of variables. Java may allow us to do so in the future, but we don't know when.

However, there are strong reasons for limiting the scope of the inferred variables, to spot the errors due to mismatch of assumptions and the actual, early on. The contracts of the public APIs should be explicit. Type inference with public APIs would allow for these errors to be caught and corrected much later.

 The contract of the public APIs should be explicit; they shouldn't depend on type inference.

The following is a practical example of how a mismatch between an assumption and the actual case can lead to errors.

Recently, my daughter was traveling overseas with her school for a student exchange program. The school asked me to send back a set of photographs for her visa application. I called a photographer, requesting that he print photos for the visa (and specifying the country). Two days later, the school asked me to resubmit the photos because they didn't match the rules.

What went wrong? Neither the school nor myself were explicit with the specifications of the photograph. The school assumed that I would know the specifications; I assumed that the photographer would know the specifications (because he had been doing it for years). In this case, at least one person assumed that the result conformed to a specific output, without explicitly specifying the output. Without an explicit contract, there is always the chance of mismatching the expectation with the actual case.

Despite the confusion, the mistake was spotted and corrected before the applications were submitted to the embassy.

The following is a fun image, included showing why the use of type inference is limited to local variables. The local instances and static variables are competing in a race, and only the local variables can make it to the finish line:

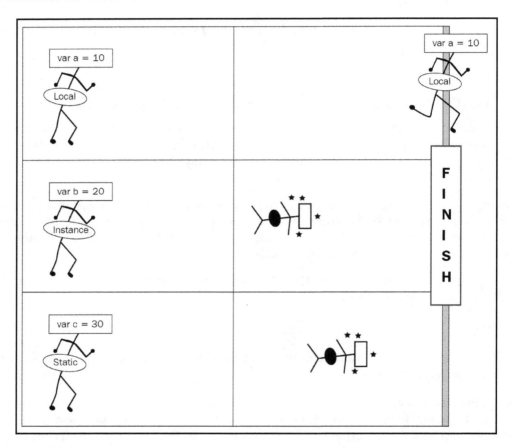

Breaking existing code

As of Java 10, `var` is a restricted local variable type and cannot be used for type declarations. Code that uses `var` as the name of a class, interface, method, method parameters, or variables, will no longer compile in JDK 10 and later releases.

The following is an example of code that uses `var` at multiple places and won't compile:

```
class var {}          // can't use var as class name
interface var {}      // can't use var as interface name
class Demo {
    int var = 100;              // can't use var as instance variable
                               // name
    static long var = 121;     // can't use var as static variable
                               // name

    void var() {               // can't use var as method name
        int var = 10;          // cant use var as the name of a local
                               // variable
    }
    void aMethod(String var) {} // can't use var as the name of method
parameter
}
```

 It is important to test your production code with the latest Java release versions, even if you are not planning to deploy your production code to them. It will help to iron out any compatibility issues with your production code, helping to migrate it to a future version of Java.

Non-denotable types

Java types that you can use in a program, like `int`, `Byte`, `Comparable`, or `String`, are called **denotable** types. The types used by a compiler internally, like the subclass of an anonymous class, which you can't write in your program, are called **non-denotable** types.

Up until now, type inference with variables seemed quite easy to implement—just get the information about the values passed to a method and returned from a method, and infer the type. However, it isn't as simple as that when it comes to inference with non-denotable types—`null` types, intersection types, anonymous class types, and capture types.

For example, consider the following code and think about the type of the inferred variables:

```
// inferred type java.util.ImmutableCollections$ListN
var a = List.of(1, "2", new StringBuilder());
var b = List.of(new ArrayList<String>(), LocalTime.now());
```

Type of variable `a` and `b` isn't a type that you would have read before. But that doesn't stop them from being inferred. The compiler infers them to a non-denotable type.

Meaningful variable names

Type inference with `var` should be used responsibly. When you remove explicit data type from a variable declaration, the variable name takes the center stage. With inferred types, it is your responsibility to use descriptive and appropriate variable names, so that they make more sense in code. As you know, a piece of code is written once, but read many times.

For example, the following line of code won't make much sense to you or to your team members (especially with a big or distributed team) after a period of time:

```
var i = getData();              // what does getData() return? Is 'i' a
                                // good name?
```

The key questions are—what is the variable `i` used for? What does the method `getData()` return? Imagine the plight of the other team members that will work with this code after you leave.

Also, it doesn't help to define variable names that are mismatched with their purposes. For example, it doesn't make much sense to create a connection object named `database` and assign a `URL` instance to it, or to define a variable with the name `query` and assign a `Connection` instance to it:

```
var database = new URL("http://www.eJavaGuru.com/malagupta.html");
var query = con.getConnection();
```

 When variables are defined using `var`, variable names become more important. Without a type, it can become difficult to understand the purpose of a variable, especially if its name is not expressive enough. Choose variable names carefully and responsibly, making their purpose clear.

Code refactoring

Type inference with `var` was introduced to reduce the verbosity of the Java language. It will help the programmers to be more concise in their methods. The compiler infers the type of the variables declared using `var` and inserts it in the bytecode. There is no need to refactor existing or legacy code, replacing explicit data types of local variables with `var`.

Type inference versus dynamic binding

The use of type inference with `var` isn't pushing Java towards the dynamic binding domain. Java is still a strongly-typed static language. The type inference in Java is syntactic sugar. The compiler infers the type and adds it to the bytecode. In dynamic binding, a variable type is inferred at runtime. This can lead to more errors being discovered later.

Summary

In this chapter, we covered local variable inference, or `var`, as introduced in Java 10. The `var` type enables you to drop the explicit data type for a local variable in a method. We covered the various dos and don'ts for the usage of `var`. Limited to local variables, variables defined using `var` must be initialized with a value. They can be used with all types of variables—primitives and objects. Variables defined with `var` can also be passed to methods and returned from methods; method declaration compatibility rules apply.

To avoid risking your type safety with generics, ensure that you pass relevant information when using `var` with generics. Although it doesn't make a lot of sense, the use of explicit casting is allowed with variables defined using `var`.

We also covered ways in which type inference existed in previous versions of Java (5, 7, and 8). Toward the end, we covered why type inference is limited to local variables and is not allowed in the public API.

The use of meaningful variable names has always been recommended, and it is important. With `var`, it becomes even more important. Since `var` offers syntactic sugar, it doesn't make any sense to refactor your existing or legacy code to add the use of `var`.

2 AppCDS

Application Class-Data Sharing, or **AppCDS**, extends the capabilities of **Class-Data Sharing** (**CDS**). It enables programmers to include selected application classes in the shared archive file, along with the core library classes, to reduce the startup time of Java applications. It also results in a reduced memory footprint.

The shared archive file created with AppCDS can include classes from the runtime image, application classes from the runtime image, and application classes from the classpath.

In this chapter, we'll cover the following topics:

- Introduction to CDS
- Creating a shared archive with CDS
- Introduction to AppCDS
- Identifying application files to be placed in the shared archive with AppCDS
- Creating and using a shared application archive file

Technical requirements

To work with the code in this chapter, you should have JDK version 10 or later installed on your system.

All code in this chapter can be accessed at `https://github.com/PacktPublishing/Java-11-and-12-New-Features`.

Since AppCDS extends the capabilities of CDS, it would help to have an understanding of CDS before starting with AppCDS. The next section introduces CDS, including where to find the shared archive file, how to create or recreate it, and the relevant commands to do so. You can skip the next section on CDS if you have practical experience of working with it.

What is CDS?

CDS has been a commercial feature with Oracle JVM since Java 8. CDS helps in two ways—it helps to reduce the startup time of a Java application and reduces its memory footprint with multiple **Java Virtual Machines (JVMs)**.

When you start up your JVM, it performs multiple steps to prepare the environment for execution. This includes bytecode loading, verification, linking, and initializing of core classes and interfaces. The classes and interfaces are combined into the runtime state of JVM so that they can be executed. It also includes method areas and constant pools.

These sets of core classes and interfaces don't change unless you update your JVM. So, every time you start your JVM, it performs the *same* steps to get the environment up for execution. Imagine you could dump the result to a file, which could be read by your JVM at startup. The subsequent startups could get the environment up and running without performing the intermediate steps of loading, verification, linking, and initialization. Welcome to CDS.

When you *install* JRE, CDS creates a shared archive file from a set of predefined set of classes from the system `jar` file. Classes are verified by the class loaders before they can be used—and this process applies to all the classes. To speed up this process, the installation process loads these classes into an internal representation and then dumps that representation to `classes.jsa`—a shared archive file. When JVM starts or restarts, `classes.jsa` is memory-mapped to save loading those classes.

When JVM's metadata is shared among multiple JVM processes, it results in a smaller memory footprint. Loading classes from a populated cache is faster than loading them from the disk; they are also partially verified. This feature is also beneficial for Java applications that start new JVM instances.

Location of the shared archive file

By default, the JDK installation process creates the class data-sharing file with the name
`classes.jsa`. The default location of `classes.jsa` is as follows:

- Solaris/Linux/macOS: `/lib/[arch]/server/classes.jsa`
- Windows platforms: `/bin/server/classes.jsa` (as shown in the following screenshot):

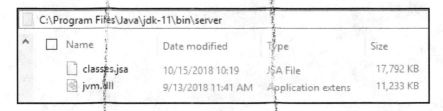

The size of the shared archived file, that is, `classes.jsa`, is
approximately 17.2 MB on a Windows system.

Manual creation of classes.jsa

This shared archive file can also be created manually using the following runtime
command (you should have enough permissions to write to the target directory):

```
java -Xshare:dump
```

Here's a sample output of the preceding command:

```
C:\Users\Mala Gupta >java -Xshare:dump
narrow_klass_base = 0x0000000800000000, narrow_klass_shift = 3
Allocated temporary class space: 1073741824 bytes at 0x00000008c0000000
Allocated shared space: 3221225472 bytes at 0x0000000800000000
Loading classes to share ...
Loading classes to share: done.
Rewriting and linking classes ...
Rewriting and linking classes: done
Number of classes 1273
    instance classes   =  1213
    obj array classes  =    52
    type array classes =     8
Updating ConstMethods ... done.
Removing unshareable information ... done.
Scanning all metaspace objects ...
Allocating RW objects ...
Allocating RO objects ...
Relocating embedded pointers ...
Relocating external roots ...
Dumping symbol table ...
Relocating SystemDictionary::_well_known_klasses[] ...
Removing java_mirror ... done.
mc  space:     8416 [  0.0% of total] out of    65536 bytes [ 12.8% used] at 0x0000000800000000
rw  space:  4034120 [ 22.2% of total] out of  4063232 bytes [ 99.3% used] at 0x0000000800010000
ro  space:  7332808 [ 40.4% of total] out of  7340032 bytes [ 99.9% used] at 0x00000008003f0000
md  space:     2560 [  0.0% of total] out of    65536 bytes [  3.9% used] at 0x0000000800af0000
od  space:  6556656 [ 36.1% of total] out of  6619136 bytes [ 99.1% used] at 0x0000000800b00000
total     : 17934560 [100.0% of total] out of 18153472 bytes [ 98.8% used]
```

As you can see from the output messages in the preceding screenshot, this command performs a lot of operations—it loads classes, links them, counts the classes that are included in the shared archive, allocates read-write and read-only objects, and a lot more.

If the file already exists, the preceding command simply overrides the existing file.

The shared archive file that you create with the preceding command doesn't include **all** the system API classes or interfaces. It includes the ones that are required at startup.

Usage of CDS

You can manually control usage of CDS by switching it on, switching it off, or putting it on automode. These are the command-line options to do so:

- `java -Xshare:off`: Disables CDS
- `java -Xshare:on`: Enables CDS
- `java -Xshare:auto`: The default mode (it enables CDS whenever possible)

Let's quickly define a class as follows:

```
class ConquerWorld {
    public static void main(String args[]) {
        System.out.println("Go and conquer the world");
    }
}
```

Let's execute the preceding class (`ConquerWorld`) using the shared archive file, `classes.jsa`. To view the system class loading from the shared archive, you can use a `log` file with class execution, as follows:

java -Xlog:class+load:file=myCDSlog.log ConquerWorld

The preceding command outputs the following:

Go and conquer the world

Let's examine the contents of the `myCDSlog.log` file (I've highlighted text to draw your attention to specific lines; the highlighted text isn't included in the `log` file):

```
[0.010s][info][class,load] opened: C:\Program Files\Java\jdk-11\lib\modules
[0.020s][info][class,load] java.lang.Object source: shared objects file
[0.020s][info][class,load] java.io.Serializable source: shared objects file
[0.020s][info][class,load] java.lang.Comparable source: shared objects file
[0.020s][info][class,load] java.lang.CharSequence source: shared objects file
[0.020s][info][class,load] java.lang.String source: shared objects file
[0.020s][info][class,load] java.lang.reflect.AnnotatedElement source: shared objects file
[0.020s][info][class,load] java.lang.reflect.GenericDeclaration source: shared objects file
[0.020s][info][class,load] java.lang.reflect.Type source: shared objects file
    .
    .
    .
[0.082s][info][class,load] ConquerWorld source: file:/C:/Users/MalaGupta/AppDataSharing/code/
[0.082s][info][class,load] java.lang.NamedPackage source: shared objects file
[0.082s][info][class,load] java.lang.PublicMethods$MethodList source: shared objects file
[0.082s][info][class,load] java.lang.PublicMethods$Key source: shared objects file
[0.082s][info][class,load] java.lang.Void source: shared objects file
[0.083s][info][class,load] jdk.internal.misc.TerminatingThreadLocal$1 source: shared objects file
[0.083s][info][class,load] java.lang.Shutdown source: shared objects file
[0.083s][info][class,load] java.lang.Shutdown$Lock source: shared objects file
```

The `classes.jsa` file is also referred to as the **shared objects file**. JVM loads approximately 500 classes or interfaces from `classes.jsa` to set up the execution environment. It loads the bytecodes of the `ConquerWorld` class from the relevant location on the system.

 If you scrutinize the `myCDSlog.log` file, you'll notice that a few of the classes are not loaded from the shared objects file. This is because they couldn't be archived; this can happen in certain cases.

Let's see what happens if you execute the same class (`ConquerWorld`) by stating that you don't want to use the shared objects file. To do so, you can use the `-Xshare:off` command, as follows:

```
java -Xshare:off -Xlog:class+load:file=myCDSshareoff.log
ConquerWorld
```

The preceding code will output the same result as it did previously. Let's examine the contents of the `myCDSshareoff.log` file:

```
[0.010s][info][class,load] opened: C:\Program Files\Java\jdk-11\lib\modules
[0.019s][info][class,load] java.lang.Object source: jrt:/java.base
[0.019s][info][class,load] java.io.Serializable source: jrt:/java.base
[0.020s][info][class,load] java.lang.Comparable source: jrt:/java.base
[0.020s][info][class,load] java.lang.CharSequence source: jrt:/java.base
[0.020s][info][class,load] java.lang.String source: jrt:/java.base
[0.020s][info][class,load] java.lang.reflect.AnnotatedElement source: jrt:/java.base
[0.020s][info][class,load] java.lang.reflect.GenericDeclaration source: jrt:/java.base
[0.020s][info][class,load] java.lang.reflect.Type source: jrt:/java.base
        .
        .
        .
[0.109s][info][class,load] ConquerWorld source: file:/C:/Users/MalaGupta/AppDataSharing/code/
[0.109s][info][class,load] java.lang.NamedPackage source: jrt:/java.base
[0.109s][info][class,load] java.lang.PublicMethods$MethodList source: jrt:/java.base
[0.109s][info][class,load] java.lang.PublicMethods$Key source: jrt:/java.base
[0.109s][info][class,load] java.lang.Void source: jrt:/java.base
[0.110s][info][class,load] jdk.internal.misc.TerminatingThreadLocal$1 source: jrt:/java.base
[0.110s][info][class,load] java.lang.Shutdown source: jrt:/java.base
[0.110s][info][class,load] java.lang.Shutdown$Lock source: jrt:/java.base
```

As you can see, since the preceding execution no longer uses the shared objects file (which was turned off using the `Xshare:off` option), the system or core API classes are loaded at runtime from their respective modules. As highlighted at the left bottom of the screenshot, you can also see that this execution takes a longer amount of time, that is, approximately **0.110** seconds. This time exceeds the execution time of 0.083 seconds for similar execution, which used the shared archive (shown in previous screenshot).

With the basic information on how CDS can lower execution time for your code, let's get started with AppCDS.

AppCDS

Increased users and usage of technology are driving exploration or formulation of better ways to improve performance every day. JEP 310 proposed extension of CDS to support application files. In this section, you'll cover how AppCDS is improving the performance of Java applications and how to create and use it.

Benefits of AppCDS

AppCDS extends the benefits of CDS to application classes, enabling you to place application classes with the shared archive of core library classes. This takes off the work of class loading, linking, and bytecode verification, leading to a reduced startup time of an application. Multiple JVMs can access a shared archive, resulting in a reduced overall memory footprint.

In the cloud, it is common for servers to scale a Java application, with multiple JVMs executing the same application. This is an excellent use case that would benefit from AppCDS. Such applications would benefit tremendously from reduced startup time and reduced memory footprint.

Serverless cloud services load thousands of application classes at startup. AppCDS will significantly reduce their startup time.

Enabling application class data archive

With Java 10, the default configuration only enabled class data sharing for JVM's bootstrap class loader. Since the bootstrap class loader doesn't load your application's files, you were expected to explicitly enable it for the application class loader and other class loaders using the following command:

```
-XX:+UseAppCDS
```

With Java 11, however, AppCDS is automatically enabled with OpenJDK 64-bit systems. When including this option, you might get an error message like this:

```
C:\Mala\code>java -Xshare:off -XX:+UseAppCDS -XX:DumpLoadedClassList=myclasses.lst -cp appcds.jar AppCDS
OpenJDK 64-Bit Server VM warning: Ignoring obsolete option UseAppCDS; AppCDS is automatically enabled
```

If you are using Java version 11 or later, you can skip this option.

 Java runtime options are case sensitive. The -XX:+UseAppCDS and -XX:+useAppCDS options are not the same.

Which application classes to archive

The next step in creating a shared archive includes specifying the application classes to be included. Examine the myCDSlog.log file that you created in the preceding section. It doesn't include each class or interface that is defined in the core Java API.

Similarly, even though your application might include a lot of classes, you need not include **all** of them in the shared archive file, simply because not all of them are required at startup. This also reduces the size of the shared archive file.

Here's an example to find the application classes that should be added to the shared archive. To start with, create a jar file of your application files.

Let's create four skeleton class files in the com.ejavaguru.appcds package:

```
// Contents of Cotton.java
package com.ejavaguru.appcds;
public class Cotton {}

// Contents of Plastic.java
package com.ejavaguru.appcds;
public class Plastic {}

// Contents of PlasticBottle.java
package com.ejavaguru.appcds;
public class PlasticBottle extends Plastic {}

// Contents of Wood.java
package com.ejavaguru.appcds;
public class Wood {}
```

And here's the content of the `AppCDS` class, which uses one of the preceding classes. It isn't defined in the same package:

```
// Contents of class AppCDS.java
import com.ejavaguru.appcds.*;
class AppCDS {
    public static void main(String args[]) {
        System.out.println(new Plastic());
    }
}
```

If your directory structure matches your package structure, you can create a `jar` file using the following command:

```
C:\Mala\code\Java11BookCode>jar cvf appcds.jar com/ejavaguru/appcds/*.class
added manifest
adding: com/ejavaguru/appcds/Cotton.class(in = 207) (out= 174)(deflated 15%)
adding: com/ejavaguru/appcds/Plastic.class(in = 209) (out= 175)(deflated 16%)
adding: com/ejavaguru/appcds/PlasticBottle.class(in = 233) (out= 171)(deflated 26%)
adding: com/ejavaguru/appcds/Wood.class(in = 203) (out= 173)(deflated 14%)
```

To determine the application classes that should be placed in the shared archive, execute the following command:

```
java -Xshare:off
     -XX:DumpLoadedClassList=myappCDS.1st
     -cp appcds.jar
     AppCDS
```

On execution of the previous command, `myappCDS.1st` records the fully qualified name (separated using \) of all classes (approximately 500) that were loaded by JVM. It includes both the core API classes and your application classes.

The following screenshot includes a few of these class names from the `myappCDS.1st` file. I've highlighted the names of two application files included in this list—AppCDS and `com/ejavaguru/appcds/Plastic`:

```
java/lang/Object
java/lang/String
java/io/Serializable
java/lang/Comparable
java/lang/CharSequence
java/lang/Class
java/lang/Cloneable
java/lang/ClassLoader
java/lang/System
java/lang/Throwable
java/lang/Error
     .
     .
     .
AppCDS
com/ejavaguru/appcds/Plastic
jdk/internal/misc/TerminatingThreadLocal$1
java/lang/Shutdown
java/lang/Shutdown$Lock
```

If you revisit the code of the AppCDS class, you'll notice that it uses just one class, that is, Plastic, from the `com.ejavaguru.appcds` package. The other classes from the same package are not loaded because they are not used. If you want to load other specific classes, you should use them in your application.

After accessing the list of application files to be included in the shared archive, you can move forward and create it.

Creating an application shared archive file

To create the shared archive with the application files, you can execute the following command in Command Prompt:

```
java -Xshare:dump
    -XX:+UseAppCDS
    -XX:SharedClassListFile=myappCDS.1st
    -XX:SharedArchiveFile=appCDS.jsa
    -cp appcds.jar
```

As mentioned in the *Enabling application class data archive* section, if you are using Java 11 or a later version on your system, you can skip using the -XX:+UseAppCDS option (AppCDS was introduced in Java 10; with Java 11, you don't need to enable it explicitly). The preceding command uses the list of class names stored in `myappCDS.1st` to create the application shared archive file. It also specifies the name of the shared archive file as appCDS.jsa.

Here's a screenshot of the output from the preceding command:

```
C:\Mala\code\Java11BookCode>java -Xshare:dump -XX:SharedClassListFile=myappCDS.lst -XX:SharedArchiveFile=appCDS.jsa -cp
appcds.jar
narrow_klass_base = 0x0000000800000000, narrow_klass_shift = 3
Allocated temporary class space: 1073741824 bytes at 0x00000008c0000000
Allocated shared space: 3221225472 bytes at 0x0000000800000000
Loading classes to share ...
Preload Warning: Cannot find AppCDS
Loading classes to share: done.
Rewriting and linking classes ...
Rewriting and linking classes: done
Number of classes 683
    instance classes   =   604
    obj array classes  =    71
    type array classes =     8
Updating ConstMethods ... done.
Removing unshareable information ... done.
Scanning all metaspace objects ...
Allocating RW objects ...
Allocating RO objects ...
Relocating embedded pointers ...
Relocating external roots ...
Dumping symbol table ...
Relocating SystemDictionary::_well_known_klasses[] ...
Removing java_mirror ... done.
mc  space:     5680 [  0.1% of total] out of    65536 bytes [  8.7% used] at 0x0000000800000000
rw  space:  2092064 [ 22.5% of total] out of  2097152 bytes [ 99.8% used] at 0x0000000800010000
ro  space:  3769640 [ 40.5% of total] out of  3801088 bytes [ 99.2% used] at 0x0000000800210000
md  space:     2560 [  0.0% of total] out of    65536 bytes [  3.9% used] at 0x00000008005b0000
od  space:  3233648 [ 34.7% of total] out of  3276800 bytes [ 98.7% used] at 0x00000008005c0000
total      :  9103592 [100.0% of total] out of  9306112 bytes [ 97.8% used]
```

Let's move to the final step—using the shared application archive file.

Using the shared application archive file

To use the shared application archive file (`appCDS.jsa`) with your AppCDS, execute the following command:

```
java -Xshare:on
     -XX:+UseAppCDS
     -XX:SharedArchiveFile=appCDS.jsa
     -cp appcds.jar
     AppCDS
```

The preceding code will use the shared application archive file to load the predefined core API classes and application classes to memory. This results in reduced startup time of user applications. The demo application used in this chapter included just four or five classes to demonstrate the process, without overwhelming you. You should be able to notice a considerable reduction in startup time for bigger user applications. Also, you can share the `.jsa` file between JVMs for a reduced memory footprint.

Summary

This chapter started with an introduction to AppCDS, which extends the capabilities of CDS to your application files. AppCDS reduces the startup time for your applications and reduces the memory footprint.

You walked through the process of identifying the application classes to be included in the shared application archive file, creating the file, and using it.

AppCDS is just one of the ways to improve the performance of Java applications. In the next chapter, you'll discover how garbage collection optimizations will help to further improve the performance of Java applications.

In the next chapter, we will look at the various optimizations introduced in garbage collectors.

3
Garbage Collector Optimizations

Java 10 offered two major improvements in the **garbage collection** (**GC**) domain. It included parallel full GC for **garbage-first** (**G1**) GCs, improving its worst-case latency. It also improved source code isolation of multiple GCs for the GC code in HotSpot, introducing the GC interface.

G1 was designated as the default GC in Java 9. G1 was designed to avoid full collections by dividing memory into the survivor, eden, and old memory regions, and by performing intermediate GCs to free up the heap. However, when the pace of object allocation is high and memory can't be reclaimed fast enough, full GC occurs. Until JDK 9, full GC for G1 was executed using a single thread. Java 10 supports parallel full GC for G1.

The creation of the GC interface is a pure refactoring of the HotSpot internal code. It isolates the source code of GCs by introducing a clean GC interface. It will enable new HotSpot developers to find the GC code, and for GC developers to develop new GCs.

In this chapter, we'll learn about the following topics:

- The GC interface
- Parallel full GC for G1

Technical requirements

To work with the code in this chapter, you should have JDK version 10, or later, installed on your system.

All code in this chapter can be accessed using the following URL: `https://github.com/PacktPublishing/Java-11-and-12-New-Features`.

Let's get started with the GC interface.

The GC interface

Imagine what happens if you are a developer working on a new GC? Or, a HotSpot developer (not a GC developer) working on modifying the existing GC code? Prior to JEP 304 or Java 10, you will have had a tough life because the GC code was scattered all over the HotSpot source code.

The objective of **JDK Enhancement Proposals (JEP)** 304 is to improve the source code isolation of GCs by introducing a GC interface. This offers a number of benefits.

Benefits

By isolating the GC source code, the HotSpot internal GC code is organized better, meeting the basic design principles, which recommend code modularity and organization. A clean GC interface will help developers to add new GCs to HotSpot with ease. GC code segregation also makes it easier to exclude a GC from a specific JDK build.

It doesn't add any new GCs or remove an existing one.

 GC code isolation and the GC interface makes it easier to exclude a GC from a JDK build.

Driving factors

Imagine that you are a GC developer and you are supposed to know all the places where you could locate the code for GC in HotSpot. If this doesn't sound scary enough, imagine how it would feel if you didn't know how to extend it to your specific requirements. Or, imagine that you are a HotSpot developer (not a GC developer), and you can't seem to find a specific code for a GC. We are not done yet—now imagine that you must exclude a specific GC at build time. These cases are represented in the following diagram:

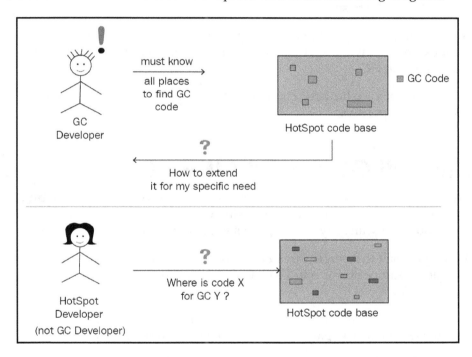

The preceding use cases demonstrate the major factors driving the changes to the code base—by pushing the creation of a clean GC interface.

Even though the code of the GCs was defined in their respective directories (for example, the `src/hotspot/share/gc/g1` stored code for G1 GC), some code was defined outside these directories. A typical example of this is the barrier required by most of the GC. Since the barrier code was implemented in the C1 and C2 runtime interpreter, this code was defined in the directories that defined the code for C1 and C2. However, this leads to a fragmented GC code, which is hard to track and locate.

A GC interface introduces a layer of abstraction, taking the burden to track all the GC code off a developer (both GC and HotSpot).

Impact

The GC interface will affect other **JavaServer Pages** (**JSPs**). It will help to deprecate the **Concurrent Mark Sweep** (**CMS**) **garbage collector** (**GC**) (**JEP 291**). With the GC interface, a GC can be isolated in the base code.

A GC interface will also help to lower the impact of the introduction of a new GC in HotSpot. For example, it will help to lower the intrusiveness of the changes made by the Shenandoah (JEP 189) GC.

In the next section, let's see how the changes with the G1 GC are helping to make applications more responsive.

Parallel full GC for G1 (JEP 307)

Imagine that you are asked to clean every nook and corner of your home, all by yourself, without any help. In this case, for how long will your house will remain inaccessible for others (since you don't want any interruptions while the cleaning is going on)?

Now compare yourself to a single thread and your house to the memory allocated to your JVM. If a single thread performs a full GC, your application will witness worst-case latencies.

G1 GC was made the default GC with Java 9, but with a single thread for full GC. With JEP 307, Java 10 makes full G1 GC parallel to improve application latency.

Let's quickly go through the details of G1, so that JEP 307 makes more sense to you.

The design goals of G1 GC

G1 GC was designed to avoid full GC collections. One of the main design goals of G1 was to add predictability and configurability to the duration and distribution of *stop-the-world* GC pauses.

For instance, with G1 GC, you can specify that the stop-the-world pauses should not be longer than x ms in a y ms time range. A real example of this is by specifying that a stop-the-world pause with a G1 GC should not be more than 8 milliseconds, every 70 seconds. The G1 GC will do its best to meet this performance goal.

However, there could be a mismatch in how you configure these values and the actual pause times with the G1 GC.

A stop-the-world GC pause refers to a state when JVM applications become unresponsive because GC doesn't allow any changes when it is marking or cleaning up memory.

G1 memory

G1 divides the memory into regions—that is, the **Eden**, **Survivor**, and **Old** generation regions—this is typically about 2,048 in the count (or as close to this as possible). A region is the memory space used to store objects of different generations, without requiring them to be allocated contiguously. The size of each region depends on the memory size. All the **Eden** and **Survivor** regions are together referred to as the young generation, and all the **Old** regions are referred to as the old generation. The size of the regions is calculated as X to the power of 2, where X is between 1 MB and 64 MB. G1 also defines the **Humongous** memory regions for large objects, whose size is greater than 50% of the size of the **Eden** regions. Since these regions are not allocated contiguously, here's how your memory might look with G1 GC:

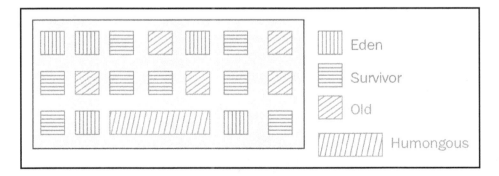

New objects are allocated in the **Eden** regions. During a young collection, a G1 GC moves the live objects from the **Eden** regions to the **Survivor** regions. Objects in the **Survivor** region are moved to the **Old** region if they have lived long enough (this is specified by using XX:MaxTenuringThreshold), or until they are collected.

A **young collection** collects, evacuates, and compacts objects to the **Survivor** regions from the **Eden** regions. A **mixed collection**, as the name suggests, will include a *select* set of **Eden** and **Old** regions. A mixed collection works by collecting objects quickly and frequently so that the **Eden** and **Survivor** regions are freed up as soon as they can be.

When an object is more than 50% of the size of a region, it is allocated to the **Humongous** region—a contiguous set of regions in the **Old** generation regions. A **Humongous** region is not allocated in the **Eden** regions in order to keep the cost of copying or evacuating it low.

When young and mixed collections can no longer reclaim enough memory, full GC occurs. This includes marking the live objects, preparing for compaction, adjusting pointers, and compacting the heap.

 This section covers just an overview of how the memory is organized and reclaimed in G1 GC so that you can follow the contents of this section. For further details, you can refer to `https://www.oracle.com/technetwork/tutorials/tutorials-1876574.html`.

Let's work with a sample code that, apart from triggering young and mixed collections, also triggers full GC, eventually exiting the JVM due to an exhausted heap and an inability to allocate more objects.

Sample code

The following sample code allocates an image array of size `999999` and loads images to it. Then, the code retrieves the image bytes and stores them to a byte array of size `999999`.

On a heap size of 3,044 MB and region size of 1 MB, this code will force full G1 GC and eventually shut down the JVM with `OutOfMemoryError`:

```
import java.io.*;
import java.awt.image.BufferedImage;
import javax.imageio.ImageIO;
public class TriggerG1FullGC {
    final BufferedImage[] images = new BufferedImage[999999];
    final byte[][] imgByte = new byte[999999][];

    public TriggerG1FullGC() throws Exception {
        for (int i = 0; i < 999999; i++) {
            images[i] = ImageIO.read(new File("img.jpg"));
        }
        System.out.println("Images read");

        for (int i = 0; i < 999999; i++) {
```

```
            ByteArrayOutputStream baos=new ByteArrayOutputStream();
            ImageIO.write(images[i], "jpg", baos );
            imgByte[i] = baos.toByteArray();
        }
        System.out.println("Bytes read");
    }
    public static void main(String... args) throws Exception {
        new TriggerG1FullGC();
    }
}
```

You can execute the preceding code using the following command:

```
> java –Xlog:gc* –Xlog:gc*:myG1log.log TriggerG1FullGC
```

The preceding code will output GC logs to the console (by courtesy of `–Xlog:gc*`). It will also store the log to the `myG1log.log` file. The code (as we expected) will fail with `OutOfMemoryError`. Let's examine the contents of the GC log file.

 Starting with Java 9, G1 is the default GC. So, the preceding code doesn't use any runtime options to specifically use G1.

G1 GC logs

In this section, we will have a look at the G1 GC logs in detail.

The following features are marked in the following screenshot:

1. Each heap region is of the size, **1M**.
2. The JVM is using **G1** as its GC.
3. The G1 collector starts a young collection 0.309 seconds after starting the application execution.
4. The G1 collector uses multiple threads for the young collection.

5. The G1 collector moves live objects from **14 Eden regions** to **2 Survivor regions**:

```
[0.012s][info][gc,heap] Heap region size: 1M ————————①
[0.018s][info][gc       ] Using G1 ————————②
[0.018s][info][gc,heap,coops] Heap address: 0x0000000741c00000, size: 3044 MB,
                         Compressed Oops mode: Zero based, Oop shift amount: 3
[0.309s][info][gc,start      ] GC(0) Pause Young (Normal) (G1 Evacuation Pause) ③
[0.309s][info][gc,task       ] GC(0) Using 4 workers of 4 for evacuation        ④
[0.311s][info][gc,phases     ] GC(0)    Pre Evacuate Collection Set: 0.0ms
[0.312s][info][gc,phases     ] GC(0)    Evacuate Collection Set: 1.5ms
[0.312s][info][gc,phases     ] GC(0)    Post Evacuate Collection Set: 0.2ms
[0.312s][info][gc,phases     ] GC(0)    Other: 1.1ms
[0.313s][info][gc,heap       ] GC(0) Eden regions: 14->0(113) ⑤
[0.330s][info][gc,heap       ] GC(0) Survivor regions: 0->2(2)
[0.332s][info][gc,heap       ] GC(0) Old regions: 0->0
[0.333s][info][gc,heap       ] GC(0) Humongous regions: 43->43
[0.334s][info][gc,metaspace ] GC(0) Metaspace: 2066K->2066K(1056768K)
```

Let's examine another section of the same GC log, as follows:

```
[1.264s][info][gc,start      ] GC(5) Pause Young (Concurrent Start) (G1 Humongous Allocation)
[1.264s][info][gc,task       ] GC(5) Using 4 workers of 4 for evacuation
[1.267s][info][gc,phases     ] GC(5)    Pre Evacuate Collection Set: 0.0ms
[1.267s][info][gc,phases     ] GC(5)    Evacuate Collection Set: 1.8ms
[1.268s][info][gc,phases     ] GC(5)    Post Evacuate Collection Set: 0.2ms
[1.268s][info][gc,phases     ] GC(5)    Other: 1.0ms
[1.269s][info][gc,heap       ] GC(5) Eden regions: 36->0(20)
[1.269s][info][gc,heap       ] GC(5) Survivor regions: 2->2(7)
[1.270s][info][gc,heap       ] GC(5) Old regions: 0->0
[1.270s][info][gc,heap       ] GC(5) Humongous regions: 148->148
[1.271s][info][gc,metaspace ] GC(5) Metaspace: 2073K->2073K(1056768K)
[1.271s][info][gc            ] GC(5) Pause Young (Concurrent Start) (G1 Humongous Allocation)
                          184M->149M(192M) 7.197ms
[1.271s][info][gc,cpu        ] GC(5) User=0.02s Sys=0.00s Real=0.01s
```

The logs in the preceding screenshot are part of the same GC collection (note **GC (5)** in the logs). It shows logs from another young collection by the G1 GC. I've highlighted the **Eden**, **Survivor**, **Old**, and **Humongous** regions that the collector worked on. The values on the left side of the arrows show the counts of regions before the collection, and the values on the right are the counts of regions after the GC.

Let's examine the last section of the G1 log before the JVM quits with `OutOfMemoryError`, as follows:

1. The collection uses multiple threads for the full collection.
2. Full GC starts.
3. Full GC includes a multiple number of steps, including marking live objects, preparing for compaction, adjusting pointers, and compacting the heap.
4. As you will notice, there are no more **Eden regions** and **Survivor regions** available for allocation and compaction (**0 -> 0**). The **Old** and **Humongous** regions contain live objects that can't be collected. As a result, the JVM shuts down with `OutOfMemoryError`.
5. This information logs the actual time taken by the full GC:

```
[20.498s][info][gc,task           ] GC(196) Using 4 workers of 4 for full compaction      (1)
[20.498s][info][gc,start          ] GC(196) Pause Full (G1 Humongous Allocation)
[20.499s][info][gc,phases,start   ] GC(196) Phase 1: Mark live objects
[20.502s][info][gc,stringtable    ] GC(196) Cleaned string and symbol table, strings: 2609 processed, 23 removed,
                                     symbols: 5461
[20.502s][info][gc,phases         ] GC(196) Phase 1: Mark live objects 3.246ms
[20.502s][info][gc,phases,start   ] GC(196) Phase 2: Prepare for compaction
[20.504s][info][gc,phases         ] GC(196) Phase 2: Prepare for compaction 1.450ms
[20.504s][info][gc,phases,start   ] GC(196) Phase 3: Adjust pointers                        (3)
[20.509s][info][gc,phases         ] GC(196) Phase 3: Adjust pointers 4.849ms
[20.513s][info][gc,phases,start   ] GC(196) Phase 4: Compact heap
[20.515s][info][gc,phases         ] GC(196) Phase 4: Compact heap 1.795ms
[20.517s][info][gc,heap           ] GC(196) Eden regions: 0->0(152)
[20.517s][info][gc,heap           ] GC(196) Survivor regions: 0->0(19)
[20.518s][info][gc,heap           ] GC(196) Old regions: 3->3                                (4)
[20.519s][info][gc,heap           ] GC(196) Humongous regions: 2983->2983
[20.519s][info][gc,metaspace      ] GC(196) Metaspace: 2114K->2022K(1056768K)
[20.519s][info][gc               ] GC(196) Pause Full (G1 Humongous Allocation) 2984M->2983M(3044M) 20.705ms  (5)
[20.519s][info][gc,cpu           ] GC(196) User=0.02s Sys=0.02s Real=0.02s
[20.520s][info][gc,marking       ] GC(193) Concurrent Mark From Roots 61.566ms
[20.520s][info][gc,marking       ] GC(193) Concurrent Mark Abort
[20.520s][info][gc               ] GC(193) Concurrent Cycle 63.136ms
[20.523s][info][gc,heap,exit     ] Heap
[20.523s][info][gc,heap,exit     ]  garbage-first heap   total 3117056K, used 3055583K [0x0000000741c00000,
                                     0x0000000800000000)
[20.524s][info][gc,heap,exit     ]   region size 1024K, 1 young (1024K), 0 survivors (0K)
[20.524s][info][gc,heap,exit     ]  Metaspace      used 2037K, capacity 4544K, committed 4864K, reserved 1056768K
[20.524s][info][gc,heap,exit     ]   class space   used 185K, capacity 408K, committed 512K, reserved 1048576K
```

The bottom of the preceding screenshot includes a few final statistics, including total heap size, used heap size, region size, and more.

Summary

In this chapter, we covered two JEPs that have brought improvements to the GC domain. JEP 304 improves the source code isolation of GCs by introducing a GC interface. It organizes the HotSpot internal GC code, enables GC developers to add new GCs to HotSpot with ease, and makes it easier to exclude a GC from a specific JDK build. JEP 307 improves the worst-case latencies of your application by making full G1 GC parallel.

In the next chapter, we will go through multiple smaller additions and modifications in Java 10.

4
Miscellaneous Improvements in JDK 10

Prior to Java 9, new versions of Java were released every three years (on average). The release timeline changed with Java 9, with the adoption of a six-month release cadence. Java 10 was released just six months after the release of Java 9. We already covered the major features of Java 10 in the first three chapters; Chapter 1, *Type Inference*, Chapter 2, *AppCDS*, and Chapter 3, *Garbage Collector Optimizations*.

In this chapter, we'll cover the remaining additions or updates to Java 10, most of which are related to changes in the JDK or its implementation. We'll also cover a few additions and modifications to the Java API.

In this chapter, we'll cover the following topics:

- Thread-local handshakes
- Time-based release versioning
- Consolidating the JDK forest into a single repository
- Heap allocation on alternative memory devices
- Additional Unicode language-tag extensions
- Root certificates
- The experimental Java-based JIT compiler
- Removal of the Native-Header Generation Tool

Technical requirements

This chapter will include an overview of the JDK 10 features that are related to the JDK or their implementation. This chapter will not include any code for you to work with.

Since this chapter covers multiple features in Java 10, let's quickly map the features with its **JDK Enhancement Proposal** (**JEP**) number and scope.

Mapping JDK 10 features with scopes and JEPs

The following table lists the JDK 10 features that will be covered in this chapter, the features' corresponding JEP numbers, and their scopes:

JEP No.	Scope	Description
296	Implementation	Consolidate the JDK forest into a single repository
312	JDK	Thread-local handshakes
313	JDK	Removal of the Native-Header Generation Tool (`javah`)
314	SE	Additional Unicode language-tag extensions
316	JDK	Heap allocation on alternative memory devices
317	JDK	Experimental Java-based JIT compiler
319	JDK	Root certificates
322	SE	Time-based release versioning

Let's get started with the first feature.

Consolidating the JDK forest into a single repository

Up to Java 9, JDK's code base used multiple repositories (there are eight repositories in Java 9—`root`, `corba`, `hotspot`, `jaxp`, `jaxws`, `jdk`, `langtools`, and `nashorn`). Consolidating the JDK forest aims to combine the multiple repositories used by the JDK into a single repository.

As JDK's code base grew over the years, it was stored in separate repositories on purpose, for a separation of concerns. However, as the JDK evolved, the code base also developed interdependencies across different repositories.

The advantages offered by these multiple repositories have outgrown the disadvantages with their maintenance. For interdependent changesets, you can't perform a single commit to a repository. There have been cases where the code for even a single (and simple) bug fix spanned multiple repositories. In such cases, the commit can't be performed atomically. A common approach is to use the same bug ID across multiple repositories. But this is not mandated, since using the same bug ID is not mandated, commits for same bug across different repositories could be made using different bug IDs. This can lead to difficulty in tracking bug fixes.

Also, the individual repositories don't have independent development tracks and release cycles. Java has one main release cycle, which includes changes in all of these repositories. Therefore, it was high time to integrate the JDK code base into one repository, to ease its maintenance.

 This is a housekeeping feature that won't affect how you write your code.

Thread-local handshakes

Suppose that you need to pause a particular thread, executing a callback on it. Prior to thread-local handshakes, there wasn't any way to do that. The norm was to perform a global VM safepoint, which pauses all of the executing threads (and what a waste that is, if you meant to pause only one thread). With thread-local handshakes, it is possible to stop individual threads.

By aiming to reduce global VM safepoints, thread-local handshakes will reduce JVM latency and improve its efficiency.

 Thread-local handshakes are a JVM implementation feature that can't be used directly by developers.

Removal of the Native-Header Generation Tool (javah)

This version of JEP has removed the `javah` tool from the tools shipped with the JDK.

Suppose that you need instances of your class to be referenced by native code in C. Developers have used the `javah` tool to generate the C header and source files from a Java class. The generated code is used to enable native code (say, written in C) to access the instances of your Java class. The `javah` tool creates a `.h` file, which defines `struct`, similar to the structure of your class. For multiple classes in a source file, the `javah` tool generates separate `.h` files.

The removal of `javah` doesn't imply any decline in the usage of your Java classes by the native code.

With Java 8, `javah` was enhanced to take on the responsibility of generating the C header and source code files. After testing over two versions, `javah` is being removed from Java SE 10.

 The removal of the `javah` tool is compensated by the advanced compilation options in `javac`, which can be used to generate the C header and source files.

Additional Unicode language-tag extensions

This feature enhances `java.util.Locale` and its related API to implement an additional Unicode extension of the BCP 47 language tag. Support for the BCP 47 language was added to JDK 7. However, in JDK 7, support for the Unicode locale extension was limited to calendar and numbers. This feature allowed for the addition of an extension to a locale. JDK 9 added support for `ca` and `nu` tags, from BCP 47.

JDK 10 added support for the following extensions:

- `cu` (currency type)
- `fw` (first day of the week)
- `rg` (region over)

When you specify a locale extension, such as a number or currency type, it is not guaranteed that the underlying platform supports the requested extension. Unicode tag extensions are a language feature, and they can be used directly by the developers.

Heap allocation on alternative memory devices

When JVM exhausts its heap memory, your application crashes with `OutOfMemoryException`. Imagine if you could configure your JVM to use an alternate memory device, like a **non-volatile dual in-line memory module (NV-DIMM)**.

With the ever-increasing memory demands of applications that deal with large amounts of data, and with the availability of low-cost NV-DIMM memory, the ability to use alternate memory devices for heap allocations is bliss. It also leads to systems that work with heterogeneous memory architectures.

This enhancement targets alternative memory devices that have the same semantics as **Dynamic Random Access Memory (DRAM)**, so that they can be used instead of DRAM, without requiring any changes to the existing application code. All of the other memory structures, such as the stack, code heap, and so on, will continue to use DRAM.

A quick detail before we move forward—NV-DIMM has higher access latency compared to DRAM. But NV-DIMM has a larger capacity at a lower cost compared to DRAM. So, the low-priority processes can use NV-DIMM, whereas the high-priority processes can use DRAM memory.

 Heap allocation is a JVM implementation detail that can't be used directly by developers.

The experimental Java-based JIT compiler

The Java compilers that you worked with until now were usually written in C/C++. What would you think about a Java compiler written in Java?

Graal, a Java-based **just in-time (JIT)** compiler, was introduced in Java 9. Java 10 enables the use of Graal as an experimental JIT compiler on Linux/x64 platforms. Eventually, Oracle will explore the possibility of using Graal as a Java-based JIT for the JDK.

Graal uses the JVM compiler interface, introduced in JDK 9. The objective of Graal is not to compete with the existing JIT compilers. It is a part of the project Metropolis, which explores and incubates Java-on-Java implementation techniques for HotSpot, the open JDK implementation of the JVM.

Since Graal is written in Java, fears of using Graal are related to lower startup performance of applications and increased heap usage.

The following command-line compiler option can be used to enable Graal as your JIT compiler:

```
-XX:+UnlockExperimentalVMOptions -XX:+UseJVMCICompiler
```

 Graal is an experimental JIT compiler that can be configured for use with command-line options.

Root certificates

Imagine configuring an account on a cloud storage service provider, using your system. The cloud interface can request a certificate and their values to be stored on your system. When reconnecting to the cloud service, your system automatically authenticates it using the certificate.

With JDK, such certificates are stored in the `cacerts` keystore. The certificate file `cacerts` resides in the security directory of your JDK installation directory and represents **Certification Authority** (**CA**) certifications applicable to the system-wide key store, as follows:

- Windows: `JAVA_HOME\lib\security`
- Linux, Solaris, and macOS X: `JAVA_HOME/lib/security`

The root certificates are used to establish trust in the certificate chains employed in the various security protocols. The problem is that the `cacerts` keystore doesn't have any certificates in the JDK source code, which is mandatory for the default functionality of security components, such as TLS, in OpenJDK builds.

With root certificates, Oracle plans to bridge the gap between the OpenJDK build and OracleJDK builds. The users must populate their `cacerts` keystore with a set of root certificates to bridge this gap.

The plan is to provide a default set of root CA certificates in JDK, and open source the root certificates in Oracle's Java SE Root CA program.

The root certificates can be issued by the CAs of Oracle's Java SE Root CA program.

 Root certificates are a JDK feature.

Time-based release versioning

The feature of time-based release versioning revises the version-string scheme of JDK SE platform, for current and future time-based release versions.

The proposed format is as follows:

```
$FEATURE.$INTERIM.$UPDATE.$PATCH
```

The following are the details of the elements used in the preceding string:

- `$FEATURE`: With the new (and strict) six-month release cadence, this value is incremented every six months. The JDK version released on Mar 2018 was 10, the version released in Sep 2018 was JDK 11. JDK 12 released in Mar 2019, and so on.
- `$INTERIM`: With the six-month release cadence, there aren't any interim releases. However, this element is retained for potential future use cases.
- `$UPDATE`: This element represents an update, incremented for compatible update releases that fix security issues, regressions, and bugs in newer features. This is incremented a month after the increment in `$FEATURE`, and every three months thereafter.
- `$PATCH`: This element represents the emergency patch-release counter, for emergency releases for a critical bug.

Summary

In this chapter, you skimmed through the various additions and modifications to JDK 10, barring its main features of type inference, application class data sharing, and garbage collector optimization.

Most of the features covered in this chapter were related to the changes in JDK, including reducing global VM safepoints with thread-local handshakes, the removal of `javah`, using alternative memory devices for heap allocation, Graal, and root certificates. It includes fewer SE features—additional Unicode language-tag extensions and time-based release versioning. The consolidation of the JDK forest into a single repository is more of a housekeeping detail.

In the next chapter, we'll look at the new additions and modifications to JDK 11. I'm excited and hope you are, too!

Section 2: JDK 11

This section starts with a discussion on lambda parameters, followed by more information on the Epsilon GC, which was introduced in Java 11. Next, we will discuss the HTTP Client API, by means of which your Java code can request HTTP resources over the network. ZGC, which was introduced in Java 11, will also be discussed in detail. Moving on, we will learn about the Java Flight Recorder profiler and the Mission Control tool for recording and analyzing data for troubleshooting. Lastly, we will have a look at the remaining features of JDK 11.

The following chapters will be covered in this section:

- Chapter 5, *Local Variable Syntax for Lambda Parameters*
- Chapter 6, *Epsilon GC*
- Chapter 7, *The HTTP Client API*
- Chapter 8, *ZGC*
- Chapter 9, *Flight Recorder and Mission Control*
- Chapter 10, *Miscellaneous Improvements in JDK 11*

5
Local Variable Syntax for Lambda Parameters

Java is enhancing its language by extending the use of the reserved type `var` for lambda parameters. The sole purpose of this enhancement is to align the syntax of lambda parameters with the syntax of declaring local variables with `var`. The parameters of implicitly-typed lambda expressions have been inferred by the compiler since lambdas were introduced, in Java 8.

In this chapter, we'll cover the following topics:

- Implicitly and explicitly-typed lambda parameters
- How to use `var` with lambda parameters
- Using annotations with lambda parameters

Technical requirements

To execute the code in this chapter, you must install JDK 11 (or a later version) on your system. All of the code in this chapter can be accessed at `https://github.com/PacktPublishing/Java-11-and-12-New-Features`.

Lambda expressions

A **lambda expression** is an anonymous function that can accept input parameters and return a value. A lambda expression can specify the types of all (or none) of its input parameters; lambda expressions can be explicitly-typed or implicitly-typed.

Explicitly-typed lambda expressions

A lambda expression that explicitly specifies the type of all of its input parameters is referred to as an explicitly-typed lambda expression. The following code illustrates a few examples (with the input parameters in bold):

```
(Integer age) -> age > 10;                      // input Integer,
                                                // return Boolean
(Integer age) -> age > 10? "Kid" : "Not a Kid"; // input Integer,
                                                // return String
(Integer age) -> {System.out.println();};       // input Integer,
                                                // return void
() -> {return Math.random() + "Number";};        // input none,
                                                // return String
(String name, List<Person> list) -> {
                            return (
                                list.stream()
                                    .filter(e ->
                                    e.getName().startsWith(name))
                                    .map(Person::getAge)
                                    .findFirst()
                                );
                        };                       // input name,
                                                // List<person>
                                                // return
                                                // Optional<Integer>
```

The code in all of the preceding examples explicitly defines the types of all of the parameters that are being passed to it. If a lambda expression doesn't accept any parameter, it uses a pair of empty round braces (()).

If this makes you wonder the types of the variables to which the lambda expressions will be assigned, here's the complete code for your reference:

```
Predicate<Integer> predicate = (Integer age) -> age > 10;
Function<Integer, String> function = (Integer age) -> age > 10? "Kid" :
                                "Not a Kid";
Consumer<Integer> consumer =    (Integer age) -> {
                                        System.out.println();
                                        };
Supplier<String> supplier =     () -> {
                                    return Math.random() +
                                    "Number";
                                };

BiFunction<String, List<Person>,
 Optional<Integer>> firstElement = (String name, List<Person> list) ->
```

```
{
                                        return (
                                            list.stream()
                                                .filter(e ->
                                                e.getName().
                                                startsWith(name))
                                                .map(Person::getAge)
                                            .findFirst()
                                        );
                                    };
class Person {
    int age;
    String name;
    String getName() {
        return name;
    }
    Integer getAge() {
        return age;
    }
}
```

Implicitly-typed lambda expressions

A lambda expression that doesn't specify the types of any of its input parameters is referred to as an **implicitly-typed** lambda expression. In this case, the compiler infers the type of the method parameters and adds it to the bytecode.

Let's modify the lambda expression from the preceding section, dropping the types of the input parameters (the modified code is in bold):

```
(age) -> age > 10;
(age) -> age > 10? "Kid" : "Not a Kid";
age -> {System.out.println();};
() -> {return Math.random() + "Number";};

(name, list) -> {
                    return (
                        list.stream()
                            .filter(e -> e.getName().startsWith(name))
                            .map(Person::getAge)
                            .findFirst()
                    );
                };
```

You can't mix implicitly-typed and explicitly-typed parameters in lambda expressions. For instance, the following code won't compile because it explicitly specifies type of x, but not for y:

```
(Integer x, y) -> x + y;                        // won't compile
```

Lambda parameters and type inference with var

In JDK 11, you'll be able to use var with lambda parameters. However, this is just syntactic sugar. The reserved type name, var, was introduced in JDK 10, to enable developers to declare local variables without using an explicit data type (to let the compiler infer the data type during compilation). But implicitly-typed lambda expressions were already doing this by using only the variable name for their parameters, without their types (examples are included in the preceding section).

Adding var to lambda parameters

Java allows for the use of the reserved word var with lambda parameters, to align its syntax with the declaration of local variables, which can now use var.

Let's modify the examples from the preceding section, adding var to the lambda parameters:

```
(var age) -> age > 10;
(var age) -> age > 10? "Kid" : "Not a Kid";
(var age) -> {System.out.println();};
() -> {return Math.random() + "Number";};

(var name, var list) -> {
                        return (
                            list.stream()
                                .filter(e ->
                                e.getName().startsWith(name))
                                .map(Person::getAge)
                                .findFirst()
                        );
                };
```

The main reason for allowing the addition of `var` to lambda parameters is to align the usage with the syntax of the local parameters declared using `var`.

If you are using `var` with lambda parameters, you must use it with all of the lambda parameters. You can't mix implicitly-typed or explicitly-typed parameters with the parameters that use `var`. The following code example won't compile:

```
(var x, y) -> x + y;                    // won't compile
(var x, Integer y) -> x + y;            // won't compile
```

You cannot enclose the parameters of a lambda expression using round brackets (`()`) if you are using just one method parameter. But, you can't drop `()` if you are using `var` with your lambda parameters. Here is some sample code to illustrate this further:

```
(int x) -> x > 10;                      // compiles
(x) -> x > 10;                          // compiles
x -> x > 10;                            // compiles
(var x) -> x > 10;                      // compiles
var x -> x > 10;                        // Won't compile
```

 You can't mix implicitly-typed or explicitly-typed lambda parameters with the parameters that use `var`.

Adding annotations to lambda parameters

You can use annotations with lambda parameters if you define them with either explicit data types or by using the reserved type `var`. Annotations could be used to mark null or non-null lambda parameters. Here's an example:

```
(@Nullable var x, @Nonnull Integer y) -> x + y;
```

Summary

In this chapter, we covered using the reserved type `var` with implicitly-typed lambda expressions. We started by identifying the syntax differences in explicitly-typed and implicitly-typed lambda expressions.

Through examples, you saw how adding `var` to lambda parameters is just syntactic sugar, since you have been able to use type inference with implicitly-typed lambda parameters ever since they were introduced in Java 8. Using `var` with lambda parameters aligns their syntax with the local variables defined using `var`. Using `var` also enables developers to use annotations with lambda parameters.

In the next chapter, we'll work with the HTTP Client API, which will be added to Java 11 as one of its core APIs.

6
Epsilon GC

Imagine that a software organization replaces its programmers with ones who don't know how to code, in order to calculate how long it will take for them to exhaust their funds and shut down. In this scenario, no new revenue is generated, while staff pay continues. In a similar manner, when you use the Epsilon **garbage collector** (**GC**), introduced in Java 11, the software application replaces its GC with Epsilon, which does not release memory—to calculate how long will it take for the **Java Virtual Machine** (**JVM**) to exhaust all its memory and shut down.

Epsilon is a **no-operation** (**no-op**) GC—that is, it doesn't collect any garbage. It only handles the allocation of memory. When the available Java heap is exhausted, the JVM shuts down.

If this GC seems weird to you, think again. The Epsilon GC has been added as a benchmark to test applications for performance, memory usage, latency, and throughput improvements.

In this chapter, we will cover the following topics:

- Why Epsilon is required
- Features of Epsilon
- Examples of working with Epsilon
- Epsilon use cases

Technical requirements

To work with the code in this chapter, you should have JDK version 11, or later, installed on your system.

All of the code in this chapter can be accessed using this URL: `https://github.com/PacktPublishing/Java-11-and-12-New-Features`.

Let's get started by exploring why we need a GC that doesn't collect any garbage.

The motivation behind Epsilon GC

You may have seen posters that state that by the year 2050, there will be more plastic in our oceans than fish. We are still in the year 2019. So, how can can marine analysts make predictions about 2050? There could be multiple ways of doing so. Perhaps they just assume that plastic is added without any cleanup, or perhaps they just use the current rate of increasing plastic pollution, or they might have applied another kind of algorithm.

The essence of this statement is that by arriving at a number (such as the year 2050), they can spread awareness about increasing marine plastic pollution. By stating that there will be *more plastic than fish*, they can get the attention of the masses and encourage them to get working now. People dread the worst; if you throw an alarming situation at them, they are more likely to react (in the suggested way).

Similarly, you could use Epsilon GC to predict the performance capabilities of your application. Because Epsilon GC can measure and tune the performance, memory usage, latency, and throughput of your applications without reclaiming the allocated memory. If you want to benchmark the application performance, Epsilon GC is the tool for you.

 Epsilon GC is used to benchmark other GCs against your applications, on multiple factors such as performance and memory usage in order to optimize your applications and use the best GCs that can work for your project.

Features of Epsilon

Epsilon doesn't clear the heap memory of unused objects; it only allocates memory. When the JVM runs out of memory, it shuts down with an `OutOfMemoryError` error. If a heap dump is enabled, Epsilon will perform a head dump, after throwing an `OutOfMemoryError` error.

Epsilon GC uses a simple, lock-free **Thread Local Allocation Buffer** (**TLAB**) allocation. This works by allocating contiguous sections of memory in a linear manner. One of the main benefits of TLAB allocation is that it binds a process to use the memory that has been allocated to it.

The barrier set used by Epsilon GC is completely empty, hence the name, **no-op**. Since it doesn't reclaim memory, it doesn't need to bother itself with maintaining the object graph, object marking, object compaction, or object copy.

Will you ever have any latency overhead with Epsilon? Yes, it is possible. Your application might experience latency overhead while Epsilon **allocates** memory—that is, if the memory size is too large and the chunk of memory that is being allocated is also large.

Latency and application performance

Imagine your application processes thousands of messages every second. In this case, a latency of even one millisecond or more can have a performance impact on your system. The worst part is that you won't even know when your GC will kick in and start the collection.

I have a suggestion; execute your application with Epsilon GC as a benchmark that won't collect any garbage. Now execute your application with GCs of your choice, and analyze the logs. Now you can filter out the latency induced due to a GC—such as GC workers scheduling, GC barrier costs, or GC cycles. The performance of your system might also suffer due to issues that are not related to a GC—such as OS scheduling or compiler issues.

GC-induced overheads versus system overheads

A GC cycle has a latency overhead. For critical applications, this can affect the desired throughput. With a carefully selected combination of multiple parameters, such as heap size, allocation units, GC cycles duration, region size, and various other parameters, you can compare the performance of your application across various GCs (including Epsilon).

However, overheads can also be induced by the system, which is not related to a GC. Executing your applications with multiple GCs will enable you to separate out GC-induced overheads from system overheads and select the best GC for your application.

By using a no-op GC such as Epsilon, you can filter out the GC-induced performance issues with OS/compiler issues.

Extremely short-lived work

Imagine that you need to create an application that is extremely short-lived. When you exit an application, JVM shuts down, and all the heap memory is reclaimed. Since executing a GC cycle takes up some time (though as little as possible), you might consider using Epsilon GC with your application.

Let's get started by using Epsilon GC with some example code.

Getting started with the HelloEpsilon GC class

Let's write a `HelloEpsilon` class and execute it using Epsilon GC. Here's the sample code:

```
class HelloEpsilonGC {
    public static void main(String[] args) {
        System.out.println("Hello to Epsilon GC!");
    }
}
```

To execute the preceding code using Epsilon GC, you must use the –
XX:+UnlockExperimentalVMOptions option with the –XX:+UseEpsilonGC option,
followed by the class to execute:

```
>java -XX:+UnlockExperimentalVMOptions -XX:+UseEpsilonGC
HelloEpsilonGC
```

The following screenshot highlights the preceding command at the top; the remaining part
includes the GC output:

```
C:\Users\Mala Gupta\code>java -XX:+UnlockExperimentalVMOptions -XX:+UseEpsilonGC
HelloEpsilonGC
[0.014s][info][gc] Resizeable heap; starting at 190M, max: 3043M, step: 128M
[0.015s][info][gc] Using TLAB allocation; max: 4096K
[0.015s][info][gc] Elastic TLABs enabled; elasticity: 1.10x
[0.016s][info][gc] Elastic TLABs decay enabled; decay time: 1000ms
[0.016s][info][gc] Using Epsilon
[0.018s][info][gc,heap,coops] Heap address: 0x0000000741cb0000, size: 3043 MB,
Compressed Oops mode: Zero based, Oop shift amount: 3
Hello to Epsilon GC!
[0.076s][info][gc,heap,exit ] Heap
[0.076s][info][gc,heap,exit ] Epsilon Heap
[0.076s][info][gc,heap,exit ] Allocation space:
[0.077s][info][gc,heap,exit ]  space 194816K,    0% used [0x0000000741cb0000,
                              0x0000000741d762e0, 0x000000074daf0000)
[0.078s][info][gc                ] Total allocated: 792 KB
[0.079s][info][gc                ] Average allocation rate: 3809505 KB/sec
```

As highlighted in the preceding screenshot, the following describes the GC output:

- JVM uses the Epsilon GC
- It outputs the `Hello to Epsilon GC!` string to the standard output
- It includes just one allocation of `792 KB`

 The literal meaning of Epsilon is an arbitrarily small amount. This aligns with its op-code.

Recently, I was delivering a session on Java 11 features, and one of the attendees had a query. He asked:

> *I understand that Epsilon GC doesn't garbage collect the Java heap, but does it garbage collect the stack memory?*

I think this is an important question. Often, we don't care about the details until we need them.

If you know the answer, this question might seem trivial to you. If not, let's answer this simple and important question in the next section.

Which memory area does GC collect – stack or heap?

JVM defines different memory management mechanisms with stack and heap memory. All GCs clean up the heap memory area by reclaiming the space occupied by unused or unreferenced objects. The GCs don't reclaim space from stack memory.

The stack memory area is used by a current thread for the execution of a method. When the current thread completes the execution of the current method, stack memory is released (without involving a GC collection). The primitives are stored on stack memory.

In a method, the local primitive variables and references to objects (not the actual objects) are stored on the stack. The actual objects are stored on the heap. The local primitive variables and reference variables that are accessible after the execution of a method are defined in the heap memory area. In essence, the following takes place:

- All objects are stored on the heap.
- The local object references are stored on the stack; the instance or static object references are stored on the heap.
- The local primitive variables and their values are stored on the stack. The instance or static primitive variables and their values are stored on the heap.

Let's work with simple use cases where Epsilon GC can help you to improve the performance, memory usage, latency, and throughput of your applications.

Memory pressure testing with Epsilon

Imagine that you don't want your application, or say, a section of your application, to use more than a certain amount of heap memory, such as 40 MB. How can you assert this? In this case, you can configure to execute your applications with -Xmx40m. Here's some example code that adds the same string values as the key/value pair to `HashMap` and then removes it—by iterating it multiple times (1_000_000 to be precise):

```java
import java.util.*;
class EpMap {
    public static void main(String args[]) {
        Map<String, String> myMap = new HashMap<String, String>();
        int size = 1_000_000;
        for(int i = 0; i < size; i++) {
            String java = new String("Java");
            String eJavaGuru = new String("eJavaGuru.com");
            myMap.put(java, eJavaGuru);
            myMap.remove(java);
        }
    }
}
```

You can execute it using the following command:

```
> java -XX:+UnlockExperimentalVMOptions -XX:+UseEpsilonGC -Xlog:gc*
-Xmx40M EpMap
```

The preceding code exits with `OutOfMemoryError`, as shown in the following screenshot:

```
[0.009s][info][gc] Non-resizeable heap; start/max: 40M
[0.010s][info][gc] Using TLAB allocation; max: 4096K
[0.011s][info][gc] Elastic TLABs enabled; elasticity: 1.10x
[0.011s][info][gc] Elastic TLABs decay enabled; decay time: 1000ms
[0.011s][info][gc] Using Epsilon
[0.011s][info][gc,heap,coops] Heap address: 0x00000000fd800000, size: 40 MB, Compressed Oops mode: 32-bit
[0.065s][info][gc          ] Heap: 40M reserved, 40M (100.00%) committed, 2M (5.08%) used
[0.071s][info][gc          ] Heap: 40M reserved, 40M (100.00%) committed, 4M (10.92%) used
[0.080s][info][gc          ] Heap: 40M reserved, 40M (100.00%) committed, 6M (17.05%) used
[0.083s][info][gc          ] Heap: 40M reserved, 40M (100.00%) committed, 8M (22.05%) used
[0.086s][info][gc          ] Heap: 40M reserved, 40M (100.00%) committed, 10M (27.05%) used
[0.088s][info][gc          ] Heap: 40M reserved, 40M (100.00%) committed, 12M (32.05%) used
[0.093s][info][gc          ] Heap: 40M reserved, 40M (100.00%) committed, 14M (37.05%) used
[0.095s][info][gc          ] Heap: 40M reserved, 40M (100.00%) committed, 16M (42.05%) used
[0.100s][info][gc          ] Heap: 40M reserved, 40M (100.00%) committed, 18M (47.05%) used
[0.103s][info][gc          ] Heap: 40M reserved, 40M (100.00%) committed, 20M (52.05%) used
[0.105s][info][gc          ] Heap: 40M reserved, 40M (100.00%) committed, 22M (57.05%) used
[0.109s][info][gc          ] Heap: 40M reserved, 40M (100.00%) committed, 24M (62.05%) used
[0.113s][info][gc          ] Heap: 40M reserved, 40M (100.00%) committed, 26M (67.05%) used
[0.114s][info][gc          ] Heap: 40M reserved, 40M (100.00%) committed, 28M (72.05%) used
[0.116s][info][gc          ] Heap: 40M reserved, 40M (100.00%) committed, 30M (77.05%) used
[0.118s][info][gc          ] Heap: 40M reserved, 40M (100.00%) committed, 32M (82.05%) used
[0.120s][info][gc          ] Heap: 40M reserved, 40M (100.00%) committed, 34M (87.05%) used
[0.123s][info][gc          ] Heap: 40M reserved, 40M (100.00%) committed, 36M (92.05%) used
[0.125s][info][gc          ] Heap: 40M reserved, 40M (100.00%) committed, 38M (97.05%) used
Terminating due to java.lang.OutOfMemoryError: Java heap space
```

Let's revisit the code that generated this output and check whether we can do something about it. At present, the code uses the `new` operator to create the same string values. Let's see what happens if I modify it to use the string pool, as follows:

```java
import java.util.*;
class EpMap {
    public static void main(String args[]) {
        Map<String, String> myMap = new HashMap<String, String>();
        int size = 1_000_000;
        for(int i = 0; i < size; i++) {
            String java = "Java";
            String eJavaGuru = "eJavaGuru.com";
            myMap.put(java, eJavaGuru);
            myMap.remove(java);
        }
    }
}
```

On the execution of this modified code, try executing the following command:

```
> java -XX:+UnlockExperimentalVMOptions -XX:+UseEpsilonGC -Xlog:gc*
-Xmx40M EpMap
```

The preceding code doesn't exit with `OutOfMemoryError` and completes the execution, as demonstrated in the following screenshot:

```
[0.011s][info][gc] Non-resizeable heap; start/max: 40M
[0.012s][info][gc] Using TLAB allocation; max: 4096K
[0.013s][info][gc] Elastic TLABs enabled; elasticity: 1.10x
[0.013s][info][gc] Elastic TLABs decay enabled; decay time: 1000ms
[0.013s][info][gc] Using Epsilon
[0.013s][info][gc,heap,coops] Heap address: 0x00000000fd800000, size: 40 MB, Compressed Oops mode: 32-bit
[0.068s][info][gc           ] Heap: 40M reserved, 40M (100.00%) committed, 2M (5.08%) used
[0.078s][info][gc           ] Heap: 40M reserved, 40M (100.00%) committed, 4M (10.92%) used
[0.083s][info][gc           ] Heap: 40M reserved, 40M (100.00%) committed, 6M (17.05%) used
[0.090s][info][gc           ] Heap: 40M reserved, 40M (100.00%) committed, 8M (22.05%) used
[0.096s][info][gc           ] Heap: 40M reserved, 40M (100.00%) committed, 10M (27.05%) used
[0.100s][info][gc           ] Heap: 40M reserved, 40M (100.00%) committed, 12M (32.05%) used
[0.104s][info][gc           ] Heap: 40M reserved, 40M (100.00%) committed, 14M (37.05%) used
[0.105s][info][gc           ] Heap: 40M reserved, 40M (100.00%) committed, 16M (42.05%) used
[0.107s][info][gc           ] Heap: 40M reserved, 40M (100.00%) committed, 18M (47.05%) used
[0.108s][info][gc           ] Heap: 40M reserved, 40M (100.00%) committed, 20M (52.05%) used
[0.110s][info][gc           ] Heap: 40M reserved, 40M (100.00%) committed, 22M (57.05%) used
[0.112s][info][gc           ] Heap: 40M reserved, 40M (100.00%) committed, 24M (62.05%) used
[0.114s][info][gc           ] Heap: 40M reserved, 40M (100.00%) committed, 26M (67.05%) used
[0.116s][info][gc           ] Heap: 40M reserved, 40M (100.00%) committed, 28M (72.05%) used
[0.118s][info][gc           ] Heap: 40M reserved, 40M (100.00%) committed, 30M (77.05%) used
[0.119s][info][gc,heap,exit ] Heap
[0.119s][info][gc,heap,exit ] Epsilon Heap
[0.120s][info][gc,heap,exit ] Allocation space:
[0.120s][info][gc,heap,exit ]  space 40960K, 78% used [0x00000000fd800000, 0x00000000ff752018, 0x00000001
[0.120s][info][gc           ] Total allocated: 32072 KB
[0.120s][info][gc           ] Average allocation rate: 100510197 KB/sec
```

 Reducing garbage is just one of the solutions to out of memory errors. To prevent or delay a GC cycle, you can also tune your runtime using multiple parameters—such as increasing the heap size or by setting a minimum time before a GC cycle runs.

This brings me to a very interesting case; can you design a garbage-free application, that is, one that can work with Epsilon forever? I think we already have a few that are in production and are in use by developers (as covered in the next section).

Designing a garbage-free application

In *Which memory area does GC collect – stack or heap?* section, I mentioned that a GC reclaims heap memory—which can include (non-local) primitive data types or objects. In your Java application, heap memory can be used by these variables and objects from either of the following:

- Third-party libraries used by your application
- A JDK API
- Your application classes

There are multiple ways to reduce garbage creation—by preferring primitive data over objects, reusing buffers, using object pools, dumping temporary object creation, and others.

Here's proof that this is possible. One of the most popular garbage-free applications Log4j, which is a logging application by Apache, runs by default in a so-called garbage-free mode. This means that it reuses objects and buffers and avoids the allocation of temporary objects as much as possible. It also has a so-called low garbage mode; this mode is not entirely garbage free, but it also does not use ThreadLocal fields. You can visit `https://logging.apache.org/log4j/2.x/manual/garbagefree.html` to learn more about it.

VM interface testing

Java 10 has added a GC interface—to provide a clean GC development interface so that GC developers and HotSpot developers don't struggle to develop new GCs, and can locate the functionality of existing GCs with ease.

To a certain extent, Epsilon validates the GC interface. Since it doesn't reclaim memory, it doesn't really need to implement the methods that require it to maintain objects to reclaim, remove, or copy them. So, it can just inherit the default implementation (which isn't supposed to do any work). Since it works, Epsilon has helped in testing VM interfaces.

Summary

In this chapter, we covered Epsilon, a no-op GC that only allocates memory and doesn't free up the heap.

You can execute your applications with Epsilon and other GCs to measure your application's performance, memory usage, latency, and throughput—eventually using the best possible combinations—tuning your runtime environment and optimizing your applications.

In the next chapter, you'll get to work with one of the most exciting features of Java—the HTTP Client, which uses reactive streams to access resources over a network in a non-synchronous and non-blocking manner.

The HTTP Client API

7

With the HTTP Client API, your Java code can request HTTP resources over the network, using the HTTP/2 protocol, in a non-blocking and asynchronous way. It brings major improvements to the existing `HttpURLConnection` class, which was added to Java in Version 1.1, and only works in a blocking and synchronous way.

The HTTP Client was incubated in Java 9, with multiple modifications in Java 10, and was standardized in Java 11. It resides in the `java.net.http` package and module.

In this chapter, we'll cover the following topics:

- An introduction to the HTTP Client
- Sending requests synchronously and asynchronously
- Converting response bytes to high-level formats
- Using Reactive Streams to handle HTTP requests and responses
- `BodyHandler`, `BodyPublisher`, and `BodySubscriber`

Technical requirements

The code in this chapter will use the standardized HTTP Client API classes from Java 11. If you are using the incubated HTTP Client from the previous Java versions, such as 9 or 10, all of the code in this chapter won't work as specified. A lot of method names have changed.

All of the code in this chapter can be accessed at `https://github.com/PacktPublishing/Java-11-and-12-New-Features`.

Before diving into the details, let's get a hang of the problem that led to the introduction of this new API for requesting HTTP resources.

A quick flashback

The HTTP Client API was incubated in Java 9. Essentially, this means that this API wasn't a part of the Java SE. It was defined in the `jdk.incubator.httpclient` package. The incubated features should explicitly be added to a project's classpath. The incubated features are released by Oracle to enable developers to use and experiment with them and provide their feedback, which decides the fate of HTTP Client API. In a future Java version, incubated APIs and features are either included as a full feature or just dropped off. There is no partial inclusion.

Just in case you need a quick refresher on HTTP, we will provide one here.

What can you do with HTTP?

HTTP is a protocol to transfer hypertext (remember <html>?) on the **World Wide Web** (**WWW**). If you have used a web browser to access any website (chances are that you have), then you've already used HTTP. Your web browser works as a client on your system, requesting access to resources, such as web pages or files, over the network. Your web browser uses HTTP to send the request to the server. The requested resources are transferred from the server to the client, using the HTTP protocol.

The most common HTTP operations are GET, POST, PUT, and DELETE. Here are a few quick examples:

- Imagine registration on a website; you fill in your details and submit them. This is a POST request, in which the form values are not appended to the URI.
- Now, imagine bookmarking the details page of your favorite book in an online portal (say, `https://www.amazon.co.uk/`). You'll notice a set of variable names and values appended to the URI (separated by &) following the question mark (?). There's an example at `https://www.amazon.co.uk/s/ref=nb_sb_noss?url= search-alias%3Dapsfield-keywords=mala+oca+8`. This is a GET request.
- The PUT request is used to create or update an entity on a server, using a URI. The PUT request refers to the entity, whereas a POST request refers to a resource that will handle the submitted data.
- The DELETE request can delete an entity, using an identifying ID appended to a URI.

Don't worry if you couldn't follow all of the HTTP operations, such as GET, POST, PUT, or DELETE. You'll be able to follow them as you progress with the chapter.

In the same way that you can access resources over the network by using a web browser, you can use your Java code to access the same resources programmatically. There are multiple use cases; for example, imagine connecting to a website, downloading the latest news and simply listing it for the users of your application.

More information on HTTP/2 can be accessed at https://tools.ietf.org/html/rfc7540.

The need for the HTTP Client API

Until now, Java developers have been using the HttpURLConnection class to request HTTP resources over the network. However, it has multiple downsides, which led to the development of the HTTP Client API.

Introduced in JDK 1.1, the HttpURLConnection class was never designed to work in an asynchronous way; it works in a blocking mode only. This contrasts with the changing nature of the applications and the data that we work with today. The world is moving toward responsive programming, which deals with processing real-time data, and we can't afford to work with blocking communications or one request or response over a connection.

The HttpURLConnection class is also difficult to use for the developers; part of its behavior is not documented. The base class of HttpURLConnection, that is, the URLConnection API, supports multiple protocols, most of which are not used now (for example, Gopher). This API doesn't support HTTP/2, since it was created way earlier than the formulation of HTTP/2.

Also, similar advanced APIs were available, such as Apache HttpClient, Eclipse Netty and Jetty, and others. It was high time that Oracle updated its own HTTP access API, keeping pace with the development and supporting its developers. One of the main goals of the HTTP Client is to have its memory consumption and performance on par with Apache HttpClient, Netty, and Jetty.

`HttpURLConnection` can't work in an asynchronous, non-blocking manner, which was one of the main reasons for the creation of the HTTP Client.

Now that you know why you need the HTTP Client API, let's get to work with its usage.

HTTP Client usage

You can use the HTTP Client to access HTTP resources across the network, using either HTTP/1.1 or HTTP/2, sending a request and accepting responses asynchronously, in a non-blocking manner. It uses Reactive Streams to work asynchronously with requests and responses.

It can also be used to send requests and receive responses synchronously.

The HTTP Client API consists of three main classes or interfaces:

- The `HttpClient` class
- The `HttpRequest` class
- The `HttpResponse` interface

The `HttpClient` class is used to send a request and retrieve the corresponding responses; `HttpRequest` encapsulates the details of the requested resource, including the request URI. The `HttpResponse` class encapsulates the response from the server.

 In Java 11, the standardized HTTP Client is defined in the `java.net.http` module and package.

A basic example

Before diving into the details of the individual classes of the HTTP Client, I'm including a basic example to let you get a hang of sending a request to a server and processing the response using the HTTP Client. I'll add to this example as we move forward, covering `HttpClient`, `HttpRequest`, and `HttpResponse` in detail. This is to help you get the bigger picture and then dive into the details.

The following example shows how to create a basic `HttpClient` instance, use it to access a URI encapsulated by `HttpRequest`, and process the response, accessible as a `HttpResponse` instance:

```
// basic HttpClient instance
HttpClient client = HttpClient.newHttpClient();

// Using builder pattern to get a basic HttpRequest instance with just
//the URI
HttpRequest request = HttpRequest.newBuilder()
                    .uri(URI.create("http://www.ejavaguru.com/"))
                    .build();

// response instance not created using a builder.
// HttpClient sends HttpRequests and makes HttpResponse available
HttpResponse<String> response = client.send(request,
                            HttpResponse.BodyHandlers.ofString());
System.out.println(response.body());
```

In the preceding code, the `newHttpClient()` factory method returns a basic `HttpClient` instance, which can be used to send an HTTP request and receive its corresponding response. `HttpRequest` is created using the builder pattern by passing it the URI to connect with (which is the minimum requirement). The `HttpResponse` instance is not created explicitly by a developer but is received after a request is sent from `HttpClient` to a server.

The `send()` method sends the request synchronously and waits for the response. When the client receives the response code and headers, it invokes `BodyHandler` before the response body is received. Upon invocation, `BodyHandler` creates `BodySubscriber` (a Reactive Stream subscriber), which receives the streams of response data from the server and converts them to an appropriate higher-level Java type.

If you didn't understand the preceding explanation completely, don't worry; I'll cover this in detail in the following sections.

 The HTTP Client uses Reactive Streams (`BodyPublisher` and `BodySubscriber`) to send and receive data streams in an asynchronous and non-blocking way. Basic familiarity with Reactive Streams is recommended in order to understand how HTTP Client sends and receives data with them.

Let's dive into the details, starting with the `HttpClient` class.

The HttpClient class

The HttpClient class is used to send requests and receive responses. It encapsulates details such as which version of the HTTP protocol to use, whether to follow redirects (if the resource you are trying to connect to has moved to another location), whether to use a proxy or an authenticator, and a few more things. The HttpClient class is used to configure a client state (an HTTP Client sends and receives data from a client to server). An HttpClient instance can be used to send multiple requests and receive their corresponding responses. However, once created, an HttpClient instance is immutable.

Creating an HttpClient instance

You can create an instance of HttpClient in two ways: by using its static getHttpClient() method, or by using the newBuilder() method (this follows the builder pattern).

The static getHttpClient() method returns a HttpClient instance with basic or default settings, as follows:

```
HttpClient client = HttpClient.newHttpClient();
```

To add custom settings, you can use its newBuilder() method, which follows the builder design pattern and calls relevant methods. Let's start with a basic version, and then add to it. For example, you can use the following code to set the HTTP version as 2:

```
HttpClient client = HttpClient.builder().
                       .version(Version.HTTP_2)
                       .build();
```

 If HTTP/2 protocol is not supported, the HttpClient instance defaults to HTTP/1.1.

Often, when you access a resource using a web browser, you see a message stating that the resource has moved to another location and that you are being redirected to the new address. In this case, your web browser receives the new URI. You can accomplish the redirection to the new URI programmatically, by specifying so, through the method followRedirects(). Here's an example:

```
HttpClient client = HttpClient.builder().
                       .version(Version.HTTP_2)
                       .followRedirects(Redirect.NORMAL),
```

```
                        .build();
```

The preceding code calls `followRedirects()`, passing `Redirect.NORMAL`.
Now, `Redirect` is a nested enum defined in the `HttpClient` class, with the following
constant values:

Enum Value	Description
`ALWAYS`	Always redirect
`NEVER`	Never redirect
`NORMAL`	Always redirect, except for HTTPS URLs to HTTP URLs

It's common for a lot of websites to authenticate a user by its registered username and
password. You can add the authentication values to `HttpClient` by using
the `authenticator()` method. The following example uses the default authentication:

```
HttpClient client = HttpClient.newBuilder().
                        .version(Version.HTTP_2)
                        .followRedirects(redirect.NORMAL),
                        .authenticator(Authenticator.getDefault())
                        .build();
```

The following code uses custom values (`"admin"` and `"adminPassword"`) for
authentication:

```
HttpClient client = HttpClient.newBuilder().
                        .version(Version.HTTP_2)
                        .followRedirects(redirect.NORMAL),
                        .authenticator(new Authenticator() {
                          public PasswordAuthentication
                           getPasswordAuthentication() {
                            return new PasswordAuthentication(
                            "admin", "adminPassword".toCharArray());
                         })
                        .build();
```

The code snippets in this section demonstrated how to create an instance of `HttpClient`.

Methods of the HttpClient class

To request an HTTP resource over the network, you'll need to call either of the methods `send()` or `sendAsync()` on the `HttpClient` instance. The `send()` method sends a request and receives its response synchronously; it will block until these tasks are not complete. The method `sendAsync()` communicates with a server asynchronously; it sends a request and immediately returns with `CompletableFuture`.

Before I include examples of the `send()` and `sendAsync()` methods, it is important to understand the other two classes: `HttpRequest` and `HttpResponse`. I'll cover these methods (`send()` and `sendAsync()`) in the section on `HttpResponse`.

Here's a quick list of the important methods of the `HttpClient` class:

Method Return Type	Method Name	Method Description
abstract Optional<Authenticator>	authenticator()	Returns Optional containing the Authenticator instance set on this client
abstract Optional<Executor>	executor()	Returns Optional containing this client's Executor
abstract HttpClient.Redirect	followRedirects()	Returns the followRedirects policy for this client
static HttpClient.Builder	newBuilder()	Creates a new HttpClient builder
static HttpClient	newHttpClient()	Returns a new HttpClient with default settings
WebSocket.Builder	newWebSocketBuilder()	Creates a new WebSocket builder (optional operation)
abstract Optional<ProxySelector>	proxy()	Returns Optional containing the ProxySelector instance supplied to this client
abstract <T> HttpResponse<T>	send (HttpRequest request, HttpResponse.BodyHandler<T> responseBodyHandler)	Sends the given request using this client, blocking, if necessary, to get the response
abstract <T> CompletableFuture<HttpResponse<T>>	sendAsync (HttpRequest request, HttpResponse.BodyHandler<T> responseBodyHandler)	Sends the given request asynchronously, using this client with the given response body handler

abstract <T> CompletableFuture<HttpResponse<T>>	sendAsync (HttpRequest request, HttpResponse.BodyHandler<T> responseBodyHandler, HttpResponse.PushPromiseHandler<T> pushPromiseHandler)	Sends the given request asynchronously, using this client with the given response body handler and push promise handler
abstract SSLContext	sslContext()	Returns this client's SSLContext
abstract SSLParameters	sslParameters()	Returns a copy of this client's SSLParameters
abstract HttpClient.Version	version()	Returns the preferred HTTP protocol version for this client

The next step is to work with the HttpRequest class to define the details of the request.

HttpRequest

The HttpRequest class encapsulates the information required to be sent across the network to the server by the client. It includes the URI to connect with, headers with a set of variable names and their corresponding values, the timeout value (the time to wait before discarding the request), and the HTTP method to invoke (PUT, POST, GET, or DELETE).

Unlike the HttpClient class, HttpRequest doesn't give you a class instance with the default values, and it makes sense not to. Imagine the URI that the client would connect to if you don't specify it.

Let's create an HttpRequest instance by calling its newBuilder() method and passing a URI to it:

```
HttpRequest request = HttpRequest.newBuilder()
                      .uri(URI.create("http://www.eJavaGuru.com/"))
                      .build();
```

You can add the timeout to your requests by using the timeout() method, as follows:

```
HttpRequest request = HttpRequest.newBuilder()
                      .uri(URI.create("http://www.eJavaGuru.com/"))
                      .timeout(Duration.ofSeconds(240))
                      .build();
```

A request instance must include the HTTP method to use. If no method is specified, a GET request is made, by default. In the preceding code, a GET request is made. Let's specify the HTTP method explicitly. The most common HTTP methods are GET and POST. The DELETE and PUT HTTP methods are also used.

The following example specifies the method as the POST method:

```
HttpRequest request = HttpRequest.newBuilder()
                    .uri(new URI("http://www.eJavaGuru.com/"))
                    .timeout(Duration.ofSeconds(240))
                    .POST(HttpRequest.noBody())
                    .build();
```

The POST method requires you to pass an instance of the BodyProcessor class. For a POST request that doesn't require a body, you can pass HttpRequest.noBody(). You can use multiple sources, such as a string, InputStream, byte array, or file, and pass it to the POST method. Here's an example that passes a file to the POST method:

```
HttpRequest request = HttpRequest.newBuilder()
                    .uri(new URI("http://www.eJavaGuru.com/"))
                    .timeout(Duration.ofSeconds(240))
                    .POST(HttpRequest.BodyProcessor
                    .fromFile(Paths.get("data.txt")))
                    .build();
```

The following example passes a string to the POST() method:

```
HttpRequest request = HttpRequest.newBuilder()
                    .uri(new URI("http://www.eJavaGuru.com/"))
                    .timeout(Duration.ofSeconds(240))
                    .POST(HttpRequest.BodyProcessor
                    .fromString("This is sample data"))
                    .build();
```

Imagine that you are working with an application that deals with buying shares when their prices rise or fall above or below a threshold. Here's some good news for you. BodyProcessor is a Reactive Stream publisher; you can deal with real-time data (such as stock prices) with controlled back pressure by using it.

 BodyProcessor defines convenient methods, such as fromFile(), fromString(), fromInputStream(), and fromByteArray(), to pass varied values conveniently.

Another frequently used method is header(), which specifies the contents of the request. Here's an example, which specifies the contents of request as text/plain:

```
HttpRequest request = HttpRequest.newBuilder()
                    .uri(URI.create("http://www.eJavaGuru.com/"))
                    .header("Content-Type", "text/plain")
                    .build();
```

Here's a list of the important methods of the `HttpClient` class :

Method Return Type	Method Name	Method Description
`abstract Optional<HttpRequest.BodyPublisher>`	`bodyPublisher()`	Returns `Optional` containing the `HttpRequest.BodyPublisher` instance set on this request
`abstract boolean`	`expectContinue()`	Returns the requests to continue setting
`abstract HttpHeaders`	`headers()`	The (user-accessible) request headers that this request was (or will be) sent with
`abstract String`	`method()`	Returns the request method for this request
`static HttpRequest.Builder`	`newBuilder()`	Creates an `HttpRequest` builder
`static HttpRequest.Builder`	`newBuilder (URI uri)`	Creates an `HttpRequest` builder with the given URI
`abstract Optional<Duration>`	`timeout()`	Returns `Optional` containing this request's timeout duration
`abstract URI`	`uri()`	Returns this request's URI
`abstract Optional<HttpClient.Version>`	`version()`	Returns `Optional` containing the HTTP protocol version that will be requested for this `HttpRequest`

Unlike the `HttpClient` and `HttpRequest` classes, you don't create instances of the `HttpResponse` class. Let's look at how you can instantiate it in the next section.

HttpResponse

When you send an `HttpRequest` instance using an `HttpClient` instance, you receive `HttpResponse`. Upon sending an HTTP request, a server typically returns the status code of the response, the response header, and the response body.

So, when can you access the response body? It depends on the `BodyHandler` that you specify to be used, when you send the request using the `HttpClient` `send()` or `sendAsync()` methods. Depending on the specified `BodyHandler`, you might be able to access the response body after the response status code and header are available (and before the response body is made available).

Let's revisit the first example from this chapter:

```
HttpClient client = HttpClient.newHttpClient();

HttpRequest request = HttpRequest.newBuilder()
                        .uri(URI.create("http://google.com/"))
                        .build();

HttpResponse<String> response = client.send(request, HttpResponse.
                                        BodyHandlers.ofString());
System.out.println(response.body());
```

In the preceding example, the `send()` method specifies `BodyHandler` as
`BodyHandlers.ofString()`. It converts the received response body bytes to a high-level
Java type: string. You can also use `BodyHandlers.ofFile()`,
`BodyHandlers.ofInputStream()`, or `BodyHandlers.discard()` to save the response to
a file, use the response as an input stream, or discard it.

`BodyHandler` is a static interface defined within the
`HttpResponse` interface. `HttpResponse` also defines a static class, `BodyHandler`, which
defines a varied and useful implementation of the `BodyHandler` interface. For example,
you could use `BodyHandlers.ofFile()` to write the received response to the specified
file. Behind the scenes, `BodyHandler` uses `BodySubscriber` (a Reactive Stream), which
subscribes to the response bytes from the server.

> The convenient static methods of `BodyHandlers` (`ofFile()`,
> `ofString()`, `ofInputStream()`, and `discard()`) let you work with a
> reactive data stream: `BodySubscriber`.

Here's a list of the important methods of the `HttpResponse` interface:

Method Return Type	Method Name	Method Description
T	body()	Returns the body
HttpHeaders	headers()	Returns the received response headers
Optional<HttpResponse<T>>	previousResponse()	Returns Optional containing the previous intermediate response, if one was received

HttpRequest	request()	Returns the HttpRequest instance corresponding to this response
Optional<SSLSession>	sslSession()	Returns Optional containing the SSLSession instance in effect for this response
int	statusCode()	Returns the status code for this response
URI	uri()	Returns the URI that the response was received from
HttpClient.Version	version()	Returns the HTTP protocol version that was used for this response

Let's work with some examples.

Some examples

What happens when you connect with a web application or web service using HTTP? The server can return text or data in multiple formats, including HTML, JSON, XML, binary, and many others. Also, the language or framework used to write the server-side application or service doesn't matter. For instance, a web application or service that you connect with might be written using PHP, Node, Spring, C#, Ruby on Rails, or others.

Let's work with some simple use cases, such as connecting to a web server using GET or POST requests, synchronously or asynchronously, submitting request data, and receiving the response and storing it using multiple formats.

Accessing HTML pages using synchronous GET

HttpClient can receive a response from a server in either a synchronous or asynchronous manner. To receive a response synchronously, use the HttpClient method, send(). This request will block the thread until the response is completely received.

The following code connects to Oracle's web server that hosts the API documentation of the `HttpClient` class, using a `GET` request sent synchronously:

```
class SyncGetHTML {
    public static void main(String args[]) throws Exception {
        HttpClient client = HttpClient.newHttpClient();
        HttpRequest request = HttpRequest.newBuilder()
        .uri(URI.create("https://docs.oracle.com/en/java/javase
        /11/docs/api/java.net.http/java/net/http/HttpClient.html"))
            .build();

        HttpResponse<String> response =
            client.send(request, BodyHandlers.ofString());
        System.out.println(response.body());
    }
}
```

The preceding code generates a lot of text. The following are just a few initial lines from the output:

```
<!DOCTYPE HTML>
<!-- NewPage -->
<html lang="en">
<head>
<!-- Generated by javadoc -->
<title>HttpClient (Java SE 11 & JDK 11 )</title>
<meta http-equiv="Content-Type" content="text/html; charset=UTF-8">
<meta name="keywords" content="java.net.http.HttpClient class">
```

The preceding code receives the HTML data as a string since it passes `BodyHandlers.ofString()` to the `send()` method. The variable used for the reception of this response is the `HttpResponse<String>` instance that matches with the response body subscriber (`BodyHandlers.ofString()`) used to process the response body bytes.

Let's see what happens if we store the response from the preceding request as a `.html` file. Here's the modified code:

```
class SyncGetHTMLToFile {
    public static void main(String args[]) throws Exception {
        HttpClient client = HttpClient.newHttpClient();
        HttpRequest request = HttpRequest.newBuilder()
        .uri(URI.create("https://docs.oracle.com/en
        /java/javase/11/docs/api/java.net.http/java
        /net/http/HttpClient.html"))
            .build();

        HttpResponse<Path> response =
```

```
        client.send(request,
        BodyHandlers.ofFile(Paths.get("HttpClient.html")));
    }
}
```

In the preceding code, the content of `HttpClient.html` is the same as the text that is sent to the console in the previous example. In this example, the response body bytes are written to a file.

Since the file is saved as a `.html` file, you can view it in your web browser. However, the display of this file won't match with the display of the hosted `HttpClient` class, because your local `.html` file can't access `.css` or other hosted styles used by `HttpClient.html`.

The following screenshot compares the rendering of the local and hosted `HttpClient.html`:

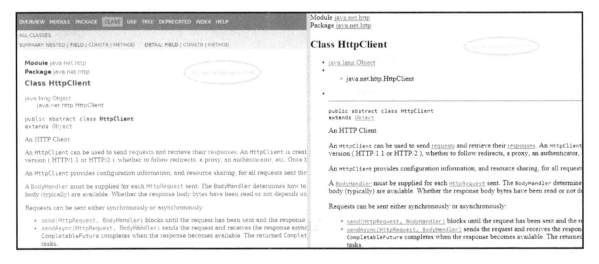

Let's modify the preceding example to receive the response asynchronously.

Accessing HTML pages using asynchronous GET

To receive a response asynchronously, you can use the `HttpClient sendAsync()` method. This request will immediately return `CompletableFuture`. You can call the `get()` method on `CompletableFuture` to retrieve the response.

Let's modify the example used in the preceding section to receive the response (HTML text) in a file in an asynchronous manner:

```
class AsyncGetHTMLToFile {
    public static void main(String args[]) throws Exception {
        HttpClient client = HttpClient.newHttpClient();
        HttpRequest request = HttpRequest.newBuilder()
        .uri(URI.create("https://docs.oracle.com/en
        /java/javase/11/docs/api/java.net.http/java/net
        /http/HttpClient.html"))
                .build();

        CompletableFuture<Path> response =
            client.sendAsync(request,
            BodyHandlers.ofFile(Paths.get("http.html")))
            .thenApply(HttpResponse::body);
        response.get();
    }
}
```

`BodyHandlers.ofFile()` is an implementation of the `BodyHandler` interface, which uses `BodySubscriber` (a Reactive Stream) to subscribe to the body response bytes. Upon receiving the response body, it writes it to the specified file.

 With the HTTP GET request, you can also include a set of parameter names and their values as a part of the URI. For example, by defining the URI as `http://www.eJavaGuru.com/Java11.html?name="Mala"`, a client can pass the `Mala` value to the parameter name.

Downloading multiple hosted image files

Imagine that you want to download multiple hosted images files without using an FTP client (or similar applications). Don't worry; you can do so by using the HTTP Client, either synchronously or asynchronously.

The code to do so is similar to what you saw in the preceding section; just save the response body bytes to a file with an appropriate file extension.

The following code downloads three hosted images from eJavaGuru (http://ejavaguru. com/) to the same folder as your source code file:

```
class MultipleImageDownload{
    public static void main(String args[]) throws Exception {
        List<URI> imageURIs =
List.of(
URI.create("http://ejavaguru.com/images/about/jbcn-actual-2018.jpg"),
URI.create("http://ejavaguru.com/images/about/iit-delhi.jpg"),
URI.create("http://ejavaguru.com/images/about/techfluence.jpg"));

        HttpClient client = HttpClient.newHttpClient();

        List<HttpRequest> imgDwnldRequests = imageURIs.stream()
                                .map(HttpRequest::newBuilder)
                                .map(builder -> builder.build())
                                .collect(Collectors.toList());

        CompletableFuture.allOf(imgDwnldRequests.stream()
            .map(request -> client.sendAsync(request,
                        BodyHandlers.ofFile(
                        Paths.get(((String)request.uri()
                            .getPath()).substring(14)
                        )
                    )
                ))
                .toArray(CompletableFuture<?>[]::new))
                .join();
    }
}
```

The preceding code uses the same HttpClient instance, client, to download multiple hosted images, by sending multiple asynchronous requests to the server. The URI instance to the images is stored in a list of URIs: imageURIs. This list is then used to create multiple HttpRequest instances: imgDwnldRequests. Then, the code calls the sendAsync() method on the client, sending the requests asynchronously.

As stated in the previous example, BodyHandlers.ofFile() creates an implementation of BodyHandler, which creates and subscribes to BodySubscriber. BodySubscriber is a Reactive Stream subscriber that receives the response body from the server with non-blocking back pressure.

Posting form details

Imagine that you want to post the details of a form to a web application or web service programmatically. You can do so by sending a POST request, using the HTTP Client API. The following code uses the send() method from HttpClient to post a set of parameter names and values to a server. The parameter names and their values are stored as a String value:

```
public class HttpReqPost {
    public static void main(String uri[]) throws Exception {
        String postData = "?
        name='Mala'&email='info@ejavaguru
        @gmail.com'";
        HttpClient client = HttpClient.newHttpClient();
        HttpRequest request = HttpRequest.newBuilder()
    .uri(URI.create("http://www.ejavaguru.com/Java11/register.php"))
        .POST(BodyPublishers.ofString(postData))
        .build();

        HttpResponse<?> response = client.send(request,
        BodyHandlers.discarding());
        System.out.println(response.statusCode());
    }
}
```

In the preceding code, the HttpRequest builder includes the following code:

```
.POST(BodyPublishers.ofString(postString)
```

The BodyPublishers class defines common implementations of BodyPublisher, which is a Reactive Stream to publish request body bytes to the server. BodyPublishers defines static methods as ofString, ofFile, ofInputStream, and ofByteArray to publish a request body from String, file, or InputStream, converting high-level Java types into a flow of data to be sent as a request body.

In this example, the POST data is stored in a string, postData, which is sent with the request to the server. In this case, I don't wish to process the received response from the server, so I use BodyHandlers.discarding() while accessing the response.

If you remember, all of the previous examples in this chapter used a Reactive Stream to receive the response body bytes from the server in a non-blocking and asynchronous manner. So, the HTTP Client enables you to send a request and receive responses to and from the server, using Reactive Streams.

The HTTP Client uses `BodySubscriber` and `BodyPublishers` to send and receive the response to and from the server asynchronously, in a non-blocking manner. The `BodyPublisher` interface extends the `Flow.Publisher` interface. The `BodySubcriber` interface extends the `Flow.Subscriber` interface.

When you work with the HTTP Client, you can also receive the response as a JSON, XML, or other data type. Similarly, you can also send multiple data types to a server. You can use the appropriate API from Java SE or another vendor to convert from one format to another.

Summary

Incubated in Java 9, the HTTP Client was standardized in Java 11. This chapter started with an introduction to the HTTP Client API, including the factors that led to its creation. Today's web applications and services should be responsive, supporting asynchronous, non-blocking data transfers. The HTTP Client uses Reactive Streams to achieve these goals.

The HTTP Client can be used to access HTTP resources across the network, using either HTTP/1.1 or HTTP/2, in both synchronous and non-synchronous manners. The HTTP Client API consists of three main classes or interfaces: the `HttpClient` class, the `HttpRequest` class, and the `HttpResponse` interface. The `HttpClient` class is used to send a request and retrieve the corresponding responses; `HttpRequest` encapsulates the details of the requested resource, including the request URI. The `HttpResponse` class encapsulates the response from the server.

Under the hood, the HTTP Client uses `BodySubscriber` and `BodyPublishers` to send and receive the response to and from the server asynchronously, in a non-blocking manner. The `BodyPublisher` interface extends the `Flow.Publisher` interface. The `BodySubcriber` interface extends the `Flow.Subscriber` interface.

The chapter included multiple examples to demonstrate common use cases.

A lot of interesting language additions and modifications are in progress as a part of Project Amber at the Oracle Corporation. We'll get started with exploring that in the next chapter.

8
ZGC

Java 11 includes a lot of improvements and changes in the GC domain. With **Z Garbage Collector** (**ZGC**), Java is bringing another GC for you—scalable, with low latency. It is a completely new GC, written from scratch. It can work with heap memory, ranging from KBs to a large TB memory. As a concurrent garbage collector, ZGC promises not to exceed application latency by 10 milliseconds, even for bigger heap sizes. It is also easy to tune.

It was released with Java 11 as an experimental GC. Work is in progress on this GC in OpenJDK and you can expect more changes to it over time.

In this chapter, we'll cover the following topics:

- Why ZGC is required
- Features of ZGC
- Examples of working with ZGC
- ZGC use cases

Technical requirements

You can use the ZGC with Java 11 and with Linux/x64 systems. ZGC is an experimental GC. All of the code in this chapter can be accessed by going to this book's GitHub repository at: `https://github.com/PacktPublishing/Java-11-and-12-New-Features`.

Let's get started by assessing why we need ZGC.

The motivation

One of the features that resulted in the rise of Java in the early days was its automatic memory management with its GCs, which freed developers from manual memory management and lowered memory leaks.

However, with unpredictable timings and durations, garbage collection can (at times) do more harm to an application than good. Increased latency directly affects the throughput and performance of an application. With eve-decreasing hardware costs and programs engineered to use largish memories, applications are demanding lower latency and higher throughput from garbage collectors.

ZGC promises a latency of no more than 10 milliseconds, which doesn't increase with heap size or a live set. This is because its stop-the-world pauses are limited to root scanning.

 ZGC is a scalable, low latency GC, which promises up to 10 milliseconds of latency, even for large heap memory (terabytes in size).

Features of ZGC

Written from scratch, ZGC brings in a lot of features, which have been instrumental in its proposal, design, and implementation.

One of the most outstanding features of ZGC is that it is a concurrent GC. It can mark memory and copy and relocate it, all concurrently. It also has a concurrent reference processor. This essentially means that you can add all sort of references, such as weak references, soft references, phantom references, or finalizers (these are deprecated now). Even then, ZGC won't add more GC pauses for you (since it will clean or reclaim the memory concurrently).

As opposed to the store barriers that are used by another HotSpot GCs, ZGC uses load barriers. The load barriers are used to keep track of heap usage. One of the intriguing features of ZGC is the usage of load barriers with colored pointers. This is what enables ZGC to perform concurrent operations when Java threads are running, such as object relocation or relocation set selection.

ZGC is a region-based garbage collector. However, if you compare it to the G1 garbage collector, ZGC is more flexible in configuring its size and scheme. Compared to G1, ZGC has better ways to deal with very large object allocations.

ZGC is a single-generation GC. It also supports partial compaction. ZGC is also highly performant when it comes to reclaiming memory and reallocating it.

ZGC is NUMA-aware, which essentially means that it has a NUMA-aware memory allocator.

An experimental garbage collector, ZGC is only available on Linux/x64. More platform support will be added in the future if there is a considerable demand for it.

Getting started with ZGC

Working with ZGC involves multiple steps. You should install the JDK binary, which is specific to Linux/x64, and build and start it. You can use the following commands to download ZGC and build it on your system:

```
$ hg clone http://hg.openjdk.java.net/jdk/jdk
$ cd zgc
$ sh configure --with-jvm-features=zgc
$ make images
```

After execution of the preceding commands, you can find the JDK root directory in the following location:

```
g./build/linux-x86_64-normal-server-release/images/jdk
```

Java tools, such as `java`, `javac`, and others can be found in the `/bin` subdirectory of the preceding path (its usual location).

Spoiler alert: You won't be able to work with ZGC unless you have Linux/x64.

Let's create a basic `HelloZGC` class, as follows:

```
class HelloZGC {
    public static void main(String[] args) {
        System.out.println("Say hello to new low pause GC - ZGC!");
    }
}
```

You can use the following command to enable ZGC and use it:

```
java -XX:+UnlockExperimentalVMOptions -XX:+UseZGC HelloZGC
```

Since ZGC is an experimental GC, you need to unlock it using the runtime option, that is, `XX:+UnlockExperimentalVMOptions`.

For enabling basic GC logging, you can add the `-Xlog:gc` option. Let's modify the preceding code, as follows:

```
java -XX:+UnlockExperimentalVMOptions -XX:+UseZGC -Xlog:gc HelloZGC
```

Detailed logging is helpful when you are fine-tuning your application. You can enable it by using the `-Xlog:gc*` option as follows:

```
java -XX:+UnlockExperimentalVMOptions -XX:+UseZGC -Xlog:gc* HelloZGC
```

The previous command will output all the logs to the console, which could make it difficult to search for specific content. You can specify the logs to be written to a file as follows:

```
java -XX:+UnlockExperimentalVMOptions -XX:+UseZGC -Xlog:gc:mylog.log*
HelloZGC
```

 When compared with G1 and parallel GCs, ZGC performs better in terms of lower latency and higher application throughput.

Let's take a sneak peek into how ZGC arranges the heap for object allocation (in short, let's start with exploring the secret sauce of ZGC).

ZGC heap

ZGC divides memory into regions, also called **ZPages**. ZPages can be dynamically created and destroyed. These can also be dynamically sized (unlike the G1 GC), which are multiples of 2 MB. Here are the size groups of heap regions:

- Small (2 MB)
- Medium (32 MB)
- Large ($N * 2$ MB)

ZGC heap can have multiple occurrences of these heap regions. The medium and large regions are allocated contiguously, as shown in the following diagram:

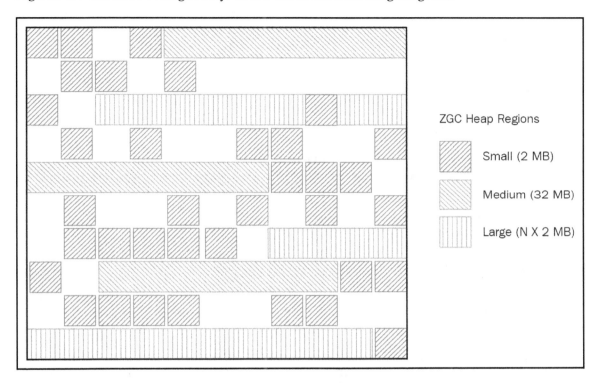

Unlike other GCs, the physical heap regions of ZGC can map into a bigger heap address space (which can include virtual memory). This can be crucial to combat memory fragmentation issues. Imagine that you can allocate a really big object in memory, but you can't do so due to unavailability of contiguous space in memory.

This often leads to multiple GC cycles to free up enough contiguous space. If none are available, even after (multiple) GC cycle(s), your JVM will shut down with `OutOfMemoryError`. However, this particular use case is not an issue with the ZGC. Since the physical memory maps to a bigger address space, locating a bigger contiguous space is feasible.

ZPages are a multiple of the same number, say, 2 MB on an Intel machine. It could vary, to, say, 4 MB on an *S* machine.

Now, let's see how the ZGC reclaims the memory from its regions.

ZGC phases

A GC cycle of ZGC includes multiple phases:

- Pause Mark Start
- Pause Mark End
- Pause Relocate Start

In the first phase, Pause Mark Start, ZGC marks objects that have been pointed to by roots. This includes walking through the live set of objects, and then finding and marking them. This is by far one of the most heavy-duty workloads in the ZGC GC cycle.

Once this completes, the next cycle is Pause Mark Start, which is used for synchronization and starts with a short pause of 1 ms. In this second phase, ZGC starts with reference processing and moves to week-root cleaning. It also includes the relocation set selection. ZGC marks the regions it wants to compact.

The next step, Pause Relocate Start, triggers the actual region compaction. It begins with root scanning pointing into the location set, followed by the concurrent reallocation of objects in the relocation set.

The first phase, that is, Pause Mark Start, also includes remapping the live data. Since marking and remap of live data is the most heavy-duty GC operation, it isn't executed as a separate one. Remap starts after Pause Relocate Start but overlaps with the Pause Mark Start phase of the next GC cycle.

Colored pointers

Colored pointers are one of the core concepts of ZGC. It enables ZGC to find, mark, locate, and remap the objects. It doesn't support x32 platforms. Implementation of colored points needs virtual address masking, which could be accomplished either in the hardware, operating system, or software. The following diagram shows the 64-bit pointer layout:

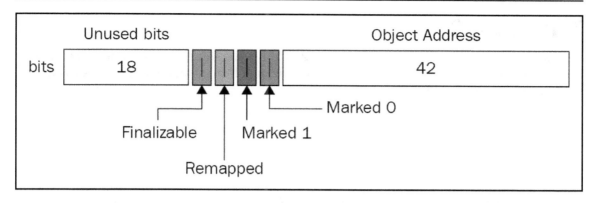

As shown in the preceding diagram, the 64-bit object reference is divided as follows:

- 18 bits: **Unused bits**
- 1-bit: **Finalizable**
- 1-bit: **Remapped**
- 1-bit: **Marked1**
- 1-bit: **Marked0**
- 42 bits: **Object Address**

The first 18 bits are reserved for future use. The 42 bits can address up to 4 TB of address space. Now comes the remaining, intriguing, 4 bits. The Marked1 and Marked0 bits are used to mark objects for garbage collection. By setting the single bit for **Remapped**, an object can be marked not pointing to into the relocation set. The last 1-bit for finalizing relates to concurrent reference processing. It marks that an object can only be reachable through a finalizer.

When you run ZGC on a system, you'll notice that it uses a lot of virtual memory space, which, as you know, is not the same as the physical memory space. This is due to heap multi-mapping. It specifies how the objects with the colored pointers are stored in the virtual memory.

As an example, for a colorless pointer, say, 0x0000000011111111, its colored pointers would be 0x0000**10**0011111111 (remapped bit set), 0x0000**8**0011111111 (Marked1 bit set), and 0x00000**4**0011111111 (Marked0 bit set). The same physical heap memory would map to three different locations in address space, each corresponding to the colored pointer. This would be implemented differently when the mapping is handled differently.

Let's explore other important JVM runtime parameters, which you can use to tune ZGC.

Tuning ZGC

Let's look at a couple of options to fine-tune ZGC (this chapter covers just a few basic ones). Let's start with the most basic option of setting the max heap size. We can do this by using the following JVM runtime option:

```
-Xmx<size>
```

To get the optimal performance, you must set a heap size that can not only store the live set of your application but also has enough space to service the allocations.

ZGC is a concurrent garbage collector. By setting the amount of CPU time that should be assigned to ZGC threads, you can control how often the GC kicks in. You can do so by using the following option:

```
-XX:ConcGCThreads=<number>
```

A higher value for the `ConcGCThreads` option will leave less amount of CPU time for your application. On the other hand, a lower value may result in your application struggling for memory; your application might generate more garbage than what is collected by ZGC. ZGC can also use default values for `ConcGCThreads`. To fine-tune your application on this parameter, you might prefer to execute against test values.

For advanced ZGC tuning, you can also enable large pages for enhanced performance of your application. You can do this by using the following option:

```
-XX:+UseLargePages
```

 The preceding command needs root privileges. Please refer to https:// wiki.openjdk.java.net/display/zgc for detailed steps.

Instead of enabling large pages, you can also enable transparent huge pages by using the following option:

```
-XX:+UseTransparentHugePage
```

The preceding option also includes additional settings and configurations, which can be accessed by using ZGC's official wiki page, hosted at `https://wiki.openjdk.java.net/display/zgc`.

ZGC is a NUMA-aware GC. Applications executing on the NUMA machine can result in a noticeable performance gain. By default, NUMA support is enabled for ZGC. However, if the JVM realizes that it is bound to a subset in the JVM, this feature can be disabled. To override a JVM's decision, you can use the following option:

```
-XX:+UseNUMA
```

Summary

In this chapter, we covered a scalable, low latency GC for OpenJDK—ZGC. It is an experimental GC, which has been written from scratch. As a concurrent GC, it promises max latency to be less than 10 milliseconds, which doesn't increase with heap size or live data.

At present, it only works with Linux/x64. More platforms can be supported in the future, if there is considerable demand for it.

In the next chapter, you'll discover how you can use **Java Flight Recorder** (**JFR**) and **Mission Control** (**MC**) to capture the OS and JVM events in a file and analyze them.

Flight Recorder and Mission Control

9

Java Flight Recorder (**JFR**) is a high-performance, low-overhead profiler that is built into the JVM. It is a data collection framework that records events that you can use to troubleshoot your Java applications and HotSpot JVM.

JFR records the events from OS, HotSpot JVM, and JDK binary events as **binary data**. This essentially means that you need a parser, such as **Mission Control** (**MC**), to make sense of this binary data.

MC is an advanced tool for program developers and administrators to analyze the data collected by the JFR profiler in detail. It can be used to analyze the data collected for applications running in local or remote environments.

In this chapter, we'll cover the following topics:

- The need for JFR and MC
- Features of JFR and MC
- Usage of JFR and MC

Technical requirements

JFR is included in the OpenJDK distributions from Java 11. Depending on which JDK distribution you are using, you might need to download and install MC separately. **Java Mission Control** (**JMC**) is not part of the OpenJDK distribution. It has been a part of OracleJDK since JDK version 7, update 40.

If JMC is not included in your JDK, you can download it from `https://jdk.java.net/jmc/`.

All code in this chapter can be accessed from `https://github.com/PacktPublishing/Java-11-and-12-New-Features`.

Let's get started with exploring why we need JFR.

The motivation behind JFR

Vaults at banks are created with near zero defects, but they aren't invincible. Imagine what happens after the vault of a bank is broken. One of the steps might include scanning the security camera footage—to check *when* and *how* the theft happened. This can lead to varied results—from determining the cause of fixing the issues and formulating measures to prevent it from happening in the future.

Similarly, you can never foresee all the challenges with your application in production. A profiler, such as JFR, helps you to record the events when your application is executing. When your application crashes or doesn't perform as expected, you can monitor or troubleshoot it, using the data collected by the profiler. This data can provide you with the feedback loop.

MC reads the application profiling data recorded by JFR and displays it *visually*, on varied values (hence saving you from wading through piles of text).

Features

JFR can record a whole lot of events—from your applications to your JVM to the OS. It is a high performance, but low overhead profiler.

JFR extends the capabilities of **event-based JVM tracing** (JEP 167), which adds an initial set of events to HotSpot, to create events in Java. It also provides a high-performance backend to write data from the events to a binary format.

MC displays the application profiling data collected by JFR in a visual environment. You can select the category you want to analyze—from class loading to JVM internals (such as garbage collection), application threads, memory allocation, to complete application data analysis. We'll work with some of the MC features in this chapter (complete coverage of all of its features is beyond the scope of this book).

Modules

JFR defines the following modules:

- `jdk.jfr`: This defines the API and internals for the JFR profiler. You can use it to profile your applications that run on resource-constrained devices such as the **IoT** (short for **Internet of Things**) or mobile devices. `Jdk.jfr` only needs the `java.base` module.

- `jdk.management.jfr`: To use flight recording remotely over **Java Management Extensions** (**JMX**), you can use this module. It requires the `jdk.jfr` and `jdk.management` modules.

We won't cover the code of JMC, just its features and how to use them.

Getting started with JFR

Let's get started with a simple `HelloWorld` example, as follows:

```
class HelloWorld {
    public static void main(String[] args) {
        System.out.println("Hello World - This is being recorded");
    }
}
```

To start flight recording for the preceding application, execute the following command on your console:

```
> java -XX:StartFlightRecording,filename=hello.jfr
  HelloWorld
```

The first line instructs the Java Runtime to start flight recording for your `HelloWorld` application and save it to the `HelloWorldRecording.jfr` file.

There are three parts to the previous command, as follows:

- Starting JFR with the `-XX:StartFlightRecording` JVM option
- Specifying the target file to save the recording to `hello.jfr`
- Specifying the application to run `HelloWorld`

Let's start MC to view the profiling data stored in `hello.jfr`. Use the `jmc.exe` file to start JMC. You'll see a window similar to the following screenshot:

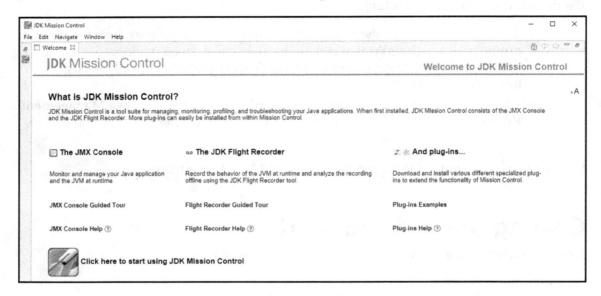

Click on the **Click here to start using JDK Mission Control** option at the bottom. Using the **File | Open** menu options, open the `hello.jfr` file you previously created. Here's what it displays at the **Automated Analysis Results** landing page:

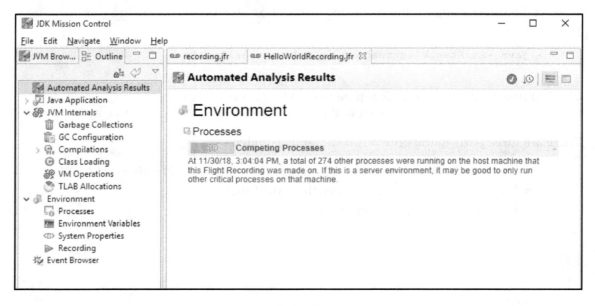

Processes are not the only category on which MC analyzes your application. Depending on your application and how it is profiled, additional categories are included.

Exploring further

Let's profile another application that creates a lot of (500) threads; each thread creates `ArrayList` of 1,000,000 `Double` values, populating it with random numbers:

```
class AThread implements Runnable {
    String name = "default";
    private Random numGenerator = new Random();
    private ArrayList<Double> list = new ArrayList<Double>(10_00_000);

    AThread(String name) {
        this.name = name;
    }
    public void run() {
        for (int i = 0; i < 10_00_000; i++) {
            list.add(numGenerator.nextDouble());
            System.out.println("Allocated : " + name + "[" + i + "]");
        }
    }
}
public class TestFlightRecorder {
    public static void main(String... args) throws Exception {
        for (int i = 0; i < 500; i++) {
            new Thread(new AThread("Thread" + i)).start();
        }
    }
}
```

Let's execute the preceding `TestFlightRecorder` application, profiling it with JFR using Epsilon GC (to check whether we also get any data on the memory allocation) for 10 seconds:

```
> java
  -XX:+UnlockExperimentalVMOptions
  -XX:+UseEpsilonGC
  -XX:StartFlightRecording,filename=Epsilon.jfr
     TestFlightRecorder
```

Here's the landing page when you open Epsilon.jfr in MC:

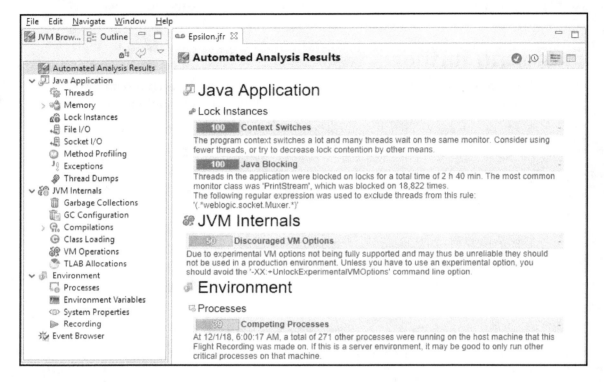

Before we discuss the results shown by MC in detail, let's quickly revisit the TestFlightRecorder application that was profiled. TestFlightRecorder creates 500 instances of the AThread class. The AThread class implements Runnable. On starting, each AThread instance creates ArrayList of 1,000,000 Double values, populates them with random values and outputs them to the console.

Let's visit the preceding screenshot now—MC displays a consolidated report on how your application fares overall. It includes the environment of the machine that is executing your Java application, the JVM internals, and blocking of threads by the locks in your application. Here's a quick listing of these categories:

- **Java Application**
- **Context Switches** (indent)
- **Java Blocking** (indent)
- **JVM Internals**
- **Environment**

Since MC reports that this application is performing poorly on the **Context Switches** and thread blocking categories, let's browse through the options under the **Java Application** category on the left-side panel menu in MC and figure out which option will include the relevant information. As you will notice, the **Lock Instances** option displays an exclamation mark right next to it. The following screenshot indicates what you will see when you click on it:

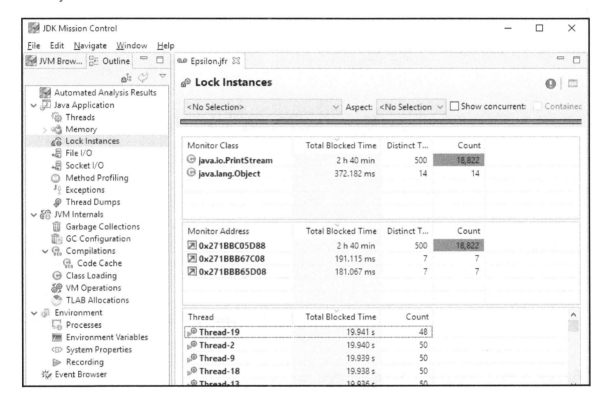

The preceding screenshot shows that all 500 threads that you created in the `TestFlightRecorder` application were blocking on `PrintStream` and `Object`. It even displays the total blocked time, that is, 2 hours and 40 minutes (calculated collectively for all blocked threads—for 20 seconds of application profiling).

Since the JFR profiler records the profiled data in a binary format to a file, you can view this data with MC at a later time and figure out a whole lot of other issues. For instance, if you click on **Processes**, you'll know that your CPU is being used by a lot of other processes that are being executed on your host machine, which can also include auto software updates. Make sure you switch all of these off. Let's say you are tuning the performance of your application on the server.

Here's what you see if you click on **Processes** in MC (of course, the results will vary across systems):

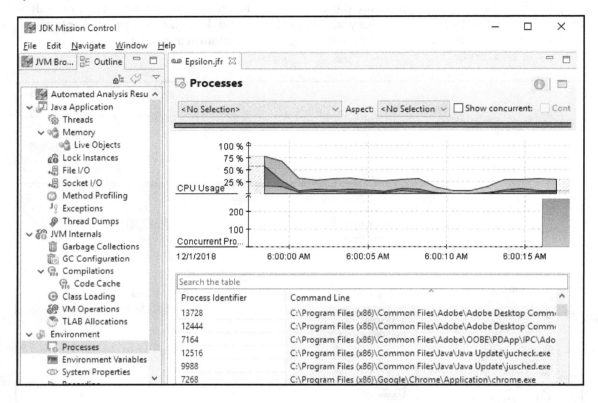

Working with custom events

As a developer, you can also create your own custom events using the JFR API and view and analyze them using MC. Here's an example; let's define a custom event:

```
class MyEvent extends Event {
    @Label("EventMessage")
    String message;
}
```

Now let's modify the `AThread` class to use events, instead of printing to console:

```
class AThread implements Runnable {
    String name = "default";
    private Random numGenerator = new Random();
```

```
    private ArrayList<Double> list = new ArrayList<Double>(1000000);

    AThread(String name) {
        this.name = name;
    }

    public void run() {
        MyEvent event;
        for (int i = 0; i < 1000000; i++) {
            list.add(numGenerator.nextDouble());
            event = new MyEvent();
            event.message = "Allocated : " + name + "[" + i + "]";
            event.commit();
        }
    }
}
public class WithCustomEvents {
    public static void main(String... args) throws Exception {
        for (int i = 0; i < 500; i++) {
            new Thread(new AThread("Thread" + i)).start();
        }
    }
}
```

You can use the same command line options to execute your application, profiling it with
JFR:

```
> java
  -XX:StartFlightRecording,filename=CustomEvents.jfr
    WithCustomEvents
```

Now, instead of using MC to view these events, you can create another application that
reads the logged events from CustomEvents.jfr, as follows:

```
class ReadFRData {
    public static void main(String args[]) throws Exception {
        Path p = Paths.get("CustomEvents.jfr");
        for (RecordedEvent e : RecordingFile.readAllEvents(p)) {
            System.out.println(e.getStartTime() +
                                " : " +
                                e.getValue("message"));
        }
    }
}
```

Summary

In this chapter, we learned about the JFR profiler. With JFR, a high performance, low overhead profiler, built into the JVM, you won't need to rely on third-party profilers to troubleshoot your Java applications and HotSpot JVM.

We also covered MC—an advanced tool for developers and administrators to analyze the data collected by JFR in detail—visually, in local and remote environments.

In the next chapter, we'll cover multiple improvements and additions in JDK 11.

10
Miscellaneous Improvements in JDK 11

Java 11 covers a number of additional interesting changes that we cannot cover in individual chapters. However, this doesn't mean that they are not relevant or important enough, but because their details are beyond the scope of this book. For instance, nest-based access includes changes to the **Java Virtual Machine** (**JVM**) specification, dynamic class-file constants extending existing class-file constants, improvements with cryptography layers and **Transport Layer Security** (**TLS**), and more.

This chapter includes an overview of the remaining JDK 11 features that are related to the SE, JDK, and implementation of Java 11 features.

In this chapter, we'll cover the following topics:

- Nest-based access control
- Dynamic class-file constants
- Improving AArch64 intrinsics
- Removing the Java EE and CORBA modules
- A key agreement with Curve25519 and Curve448
- Unicode 10
- ChaCha20 and Poly1305 cryptographic algorithms
- Launching single file source code programs
- TLS 1.3
- Deprecating the Nashorn JavaScript engine
- Deprecating the pack200 tools and API

Technical requirements

To work with the code that is included in this chapter, you'll need JDK 11, or later, installed on your system.

Since this chapter covers multiple features in Java 11, let's quickly map the features with their **JDK Enhancement Proposal (JEP)** number and scope.

Listing the JEPs that are used in this chapter

The following table lists the JDK 11 features that are covered in this chapter, their corresponding JEP number, and scope:

JEP	Scope	Description
181	SE	Nest-based access control
309	SE	Dynamic class-file constants
315	Implementation	Improving AArch64 intrinsics
320	SE	Removing the Java EE and CORBA modules
324	SE	A key agreement with Curve25519 and Curve448
327	SE	Unicode 10
329	SE	ChaCha20 and Poly1305 cryptographic algorithms
330	JDK	Launch single file source code programs
332	SE	TLS 1.3
335	JDK	Deprecate the Nashorn JavaScript engine
336	SE	Deprecate the pack200 tools and API

Let's get started with the first feature.

Nest-based access control

Imagine what happens when you define nested classes or interfaces? For instance, if you define a *two-level class*, say `Outer`, and an *inner class*, say `Inner`, can `Inner` access the `private` instance variables of `Outer`? Here's some sample code:

```
public class Outer {
    private int outerInt = 20;
```

```
    public class Inner {
        int innerInt = outerInt;        // Can Inner access outerInt?
    }
}
```

Yes, it can. Since you define these classes within the same source code file, you might assume it to be obvious. However, it is not. The compiler generates separate bytecode files (.class) for the Outer and Inner classes. For the preceding example, the compiler creates two bytecode files: Outer.class and Outer$Inner.class. For your quick reference, the bytecode file of an inner class is preceded by the name of its outer class and a dollar sign.

To enable the access of variables across these classes and to preserve the expectations of programmers, the compiler broadens the access of private members to a package or adds bridge variables or methods in each of these classes. Here's the decompiled version of the Outer and Inner classes that have been decompiled using the **JAD Java Decompiler**:

```
// Decompiled class Outer
public class Outer {
    public class Inner {
        int innerInt;
        final Outer this$0;

        public Inner() {
            this$0 = Outer.this;
            super();
            innerInt = outerInt;
        }
    }
    public Outer() {
        outerInt = 20;
    }
    private int outerInt;
}
```

And here is the Outer$Inner decompiled class, as follows:

```
public class Outer$Inner {
    int innerInt;
    final Outer this$0;

    public Outer$Inner() {
        this$0 = Outer.this;
        super();
        innerInt = outerInt;
    }
}
```

As you will notice, the decompiled versions verify that the compiler defined a bridge variable, that is, `this$0` of type `Outer` in the `Inner` class, to access members of `Outer` from `Inner`.

These bridge variables and methods risk encapsulation and increase the size of the deployed application. They can also confuse developers and tools.

What is nest-based access?

JEP 181 introduces nest-based access control, allowing classes or interfaces that are a part of the same entity but are compiled to separate class files, to access each other's private members without the compilers to insert accessibility by broadening bridge workarounds.

Nest-based access control also results in changes to the JVM specification. You can refer to the following link to access these changes (removals are highlighted by a red font background and additions are highlighted using the green background): `https://cr.openjdk.java.net/~dlsmith/nestmates.html`.

Nest-based access control allows classes and interfaces that are defined in the same source file to access each other's private members, without any workarounds (or bridge code) by the compiler.

Affects of nest-based control

Though it might seem simple, nest-based access control affects all specifications and APIs —which involve access control or method invocation—either implicitly or explicitly. As mentioned in the *What is nest-based access?* section, it includes changes in the JVM specification. It also affects class file attributes, access control rules, bytecode invocation rules, reflection, method invocation, and field access rules.

It also adds new class file attributes, modifies `MethodHandle` lookup rules, results in class transformation/redefinition—the JVM TI and `java.lang.instrument` APIs, JDWP, and JDI (`com.sun.jdi.VirtualMachine`).

Dynamic class-file constants

JEP 309 extends the existing Java class-file format, creating CONSTANT_Dynamic. This is a JVM feature and doesn't depend on the higher software layers. The loading of CONSTANT_Dynamic delegates the creation of a bootstrap method. When comparing it to the **invokedynamic** call, you will see how it delegates linking to a bootstrap method.

One of the main goals of dynamic class-file constants is to make it simple to create new forms of materializable class-file constants, which provides language designers and compiler implementers with broader options for expressivity and performance. This is achieved by creating a new constant pool form that can be parameterized using a bootstrap method with static arguments.

Improving AArch64 intrinsics

JEP 315 works by improving intrinsics on AArch64 processors. The current string and array intrinsic are improved. Also a new intrinsic is implemented for the sine, cosine, and logarithmic functions in java.lang.Math.

In order to enhance application performance, intrinsics utilize an assembly code that is specific to CPU architecture. It does not execute generic Java code.

Note that you will see AArch64 processors having an implementation of most of the intrinsics. However, JEP 315 implemented an optimized intrinsic for the following methods in the java.lang.Math class that was not up to the mark:

- sin()
- cos()
- log()

It is also worth noting that some of the intrinsics that are previously implemented in the AArch64 port might not be completely optimal. Such intrinsic can take advantage of features such as memory address alignment or software prefetching instructions. Some of those methods are listed as follows:

- String::compareTo
- String::indexOf
- StringCoding::hasNegatives
- Arrays::equals

- `StringUTF16::compress`
- `StringLatin1::inflate`

Removing the Java EE and CORBA modules

Java EE moved to the Eclipse Foundation with Java 9 under a new name – Jakarta EE (interestingly, still JEE). With Java 9, the modules and classes that were specific to Java EE were deprecated. With Java 11, these deprecated APIs and modules have been removed from the Java SE platform and the JDK. CORBA's APIs were also deprecated in Java 9 and were eventually removed in Java 11.

With Java SE 6 (core Java), you can develop web services using the following technologies:

- **JAX-WS**: Java API for XML-based web services (`https://jcp.org/en/jsr/detail?id=224`)
- **JAXB**: Java Architecture for XML Binding (`https://jcp.org/en/jsr/detail?id=222`)
- **JAF**: JavaBeans Activation Framework (`https://jcp.org/en/jsr/detail?id=925`)
- **Common annotations**: JSR will develop annotations for common semantic concepts in the J2SE and J2EE platforms (`https://jcp.org/en/jsr/detail?id=250`)

When the code for the preceding tech stack was added to core Java, it was identical to its versions for **Java's Enterprise Edition** (JEE). However, over time, the JEE version evolved, leading to a mismatch in the functionality that was offered by the same APIs in Java SE and JEE.

JEP 320 removed the following modules in Java 11, deleting their source code from the OpenJDK repository and runtime JDK image:

- `java.xml.ws` (JAX-WS)
- `java.xml.bind` (JAXB)
- `java.activation` (JAF)
- `java.xml.ws.annotation` (common annotations)
- `java.corba` (CORBA)
- `java.transaction` (JTA)

- `java.se.ee` (an aggregator module for the preceding six modules)
- `jdk.xml.ws` (JAX-WS tools)
- `jdk.xml.bind` (JAXB tools)

Apart from marking the preceding modules as deprecated in Java 9, it didn't resolve them when code that was using these modules was compiled or executed. This forced the developers to use standalone versions of Java EE or CORBA on the classpath.

After their removal, tools such as `wsgen` and `wsimport` (from `jdk.xml.ws`), `schemagen` and `xjc` (from `jdk.xml.bind`), `idlj`, `orbd`, `servertool`, and `tnamesrv` (from `java.corba`) were no longer available. Developers couldn't enable them using runtime command-line flags, as follows:

--add-modules

CORBA, an ORB implementation, was included in Java SE in 1998. Over time, support for CORBA has outweighed its benefits. First of all, with better technologies available, hardly anyone is using CORBA now. CORBA evolves outside the **Java Community Process (JCP)** and it is becoming increasingly difficult to maintain JDK's CORBA implementation. With JEE now moving to the Eclipse Foundation, it makes no sense to synchronize ORB in JDK with Jakarta EE's ORB. To add to this, JEE 8 designated it as **Proposed Optional**, which essentially means that JEE might drop supporting CORBA in one of its future versions (marking it as deprecated).

 Enterprises moving from Java 8 to Java 11 are at a higher risk if their applications use JEE or CORBA APIs. However, an alternate API is suggested by Oracle, easing the migration.

A key agreement with Curve25519 and Curve448

With JEP 324, Java SE is making further advances in cryptography that offers security and performance. This feature implements a key agreement using Curve25519 and Curve448. Other cryptography libraries, such as OpenSSL and BoringSSL, already support key exchanges using Curve25519 and Curve448.

You can find more information on Cureve25519 and Curve448 at `https://tools.ietf.org/html/rfc7748`.

Unicode 10

JEP 327 upgrades existing platform APIs to support Unicode 10 Standard (http://www.unicode.org/standard/standard.html), mainly in the following classes:

- `Character` and `String` (the `java.lang` package)
- `NumericShaper` (the `java.awt.font` package)
- `Bidi`, `BreakIterator`, and `Normalizer` (the `java.text` package)

ChaCha20 and Poly1305 cryptographic algorithms

Java 11 includes multiple additions and enhancements in cryptographic toolkits and TLS implementations. JEP 329 implements the ChaCha20 and ChaCha20-Poly1305 ciphers. Being a comparatively new stream cipher, ChaCha20 is capable in taking place of the RC4 stream cipher.

At present, the RC4 stream cipher, which has been widely adopted, is not so secure. The industry is moving toward the adoption of the more secure ChaCha20-Poly1305. This has also been widely adopted across TLS implementations as well as in other cryptographic protocols.

Launching single file source code programs

Imagine being able to execute a Java application without compilation; for instance, if you define the following Java class in `HelloNoCompilation.java`:

```
class HelloNoCompilation {
    public static void main(String[] args) {
        System.out.println("No compilation! Are you kidding me?");
    }
}
```

With Java 11, you can execute it using the following command (no compilation takes place):

```
> java HelloNoCompilation.java
```

Note that the preceding command starts the JVM using `java`, which is passed the name of a source file with the `.java` extension. In this case, the class is compiled in memory before it is executed by the JVM. This applies to multiple classes or interfaces that are defined within the same source file. Here's another example (consider it to be defined within the same `HelloNoCompilation.java` source file):

```
class HelloNoCompilation {
    public static void main(String[] args) {
        System.out.println("No compilation! Are you kidding me?");
        EstablishedOrg org = new EstablishedOrg();
        org.invite();
        System.out.println(new Startup().name);
    }
}
class Startup {
    String name = "CoolAndExciting";
}
interface Employs {
    default void invite() {
        System.out.println("Want to work with us?");
    }
}
class EstablishedOrg implements Employs {
    String name = "OldButStable";
}
```

On execution, you will see the following command:

```
> java HelloNoCompilation.java
```

The preceding code will output as follows:

```
No compilation! Are you kidding me?
Want to work with us?
CoolAndExciting
```

With JEP 330, you can cut down the step of compiling your code and go to the execution of your Java applications straight away. However, this only applies to applications with a single source file. The source file can define multiple classes or interfaces, as shown in the preceding example code.

Launching single file source code programs helps to reduce the ceremony attached to simple code execution. This is the most helpful for students or professionals who are beginning to learn Java. However, when they move to working with multiple source files, they'll need to compile their code before executing them.

However, if you compile your source class using the `javac` command and then try to launch it as a single file source code, it won't execute. For example, compile the `HelloNoCompilation` source file, as follows:

```
> javac HelloNoCompilation.java
```

Then, try to execute the following command:

```
> java HelloNoCompilation.java
```

You'll receive the following error:

```
error: class found on application class path: HelloNoCompilation
```

TLS 1.3

Here's another addition to the TLS implementation in Java. JEP 332 implements Version 1.3 of the TLS Protocol.

Version 1.3 of TLS supersedes and obsoletes its previous versions, including Version 1.2 (that is, RFC 5246, which can be found at `https://tools.ietf.org/html/rfc5246`). It also obsoletes or changes other TLS features, such as the **OCSP** (short for **Online Certificate Status Protocol**) stapling extensions (that is, RFC 6066, which can be found at `https://tools.ietf.org/html/rfc6066`; and RFC 6961, which can be found at `https://tools.ietf.org/html/rfc6961`), and the session hash and extended master secret extension (that is, RFC 7627; for more information, visit `https://tools.ietf.org/html/rfc7627`).

Deprecating the Nashorn JavaScript engine

With JEP 335, Java 11 deprecates the Nashorn JavaScript script engine, its APIs, and its `jjs` tool. These will be removed in future Java versions.

The Nashorn JavaScript engine was first included in JDK in its recent versions—JDK 8. The reason for this was to replace the Rhino scripting engine. However, Java is unable to keep up the pace with the evolution of ECMAScript, on which the Nashorn JavaScript engine is based.

The challenge to maintain the Nashorn JavaScript engine outperforms the advantages that it offers, and therefore paving the way for its deprecation.

JEP 336 – deprecating the pack200 tools and API

Introduced in Java 5, pack200 was a compression scheme for JAR files. It was used to decrease the disk space and bandwidth demand when Java programs were packaged, transmitted, or delivered. Developers used pack200 and unpack200 to compress and decompress the Java JAR files.

However, these are becoming irrelevant in today's modern storage and transmission improvements. JEP 336 deprecates the pack200 and unpack200 tools, and also the corresponding pack200 API.

Summary

In this chapter, we covered various features of Java 11. We saw how a number of changes have been introduced over different versions.

In the next chapter, we will discover the exciting new additions and modifications to the Java language as they are being worked on in **Project Amber** – which is about right-sizing the Java language ceremony.

Section 3: JDK 12

This section will show you how `switch` expressions have enhanced the traditional `switch` statement, making your code less verbose and thereby avoiding logical errors. The next chapter covers other additions and updates in Java 12.

The following chapters will be covered in this section:

11
Switch Expressions

With `switch` expressions, Java 12 is enhancing one of its basic language constructs—`switch`—to improve the everyday coding experience of developers. The benefits of this are manifold. As compared to **traditional** `switch` constructs, `switch` expressions (**JDK Enhancement Proposal (JEP)** 325—`http://openjdk.java.net/jeps/325`) can return a value. The ability to define multiple constants with a `switch` branch, and improve code semantics, make it concise. By removing default fall through of control across `switch` branches, you are less likely to introduce a logical error in a `switch` expression.

In this chapter, you'll cover the following topics:

- Issues with existing `switch` statements
- The `switch` expression syntax
- Defining local variables in `switch` branches
- The extended `break` statement
- Comparing `break` with `break <return value>`
- Exhaustive cases
- A preview language feature
- Using `return` and `continue` in `switch` expressions

Technical requirements

To compile and execute the code included in this chapter, install JDK 12 on your system. All code in this chapter can be accessed using the following URL: `https://github.com/PacktPublishing/Java-11-and-12-New-Features`.

Let's get started by covering the issues with existing `switch` statements.

Issues with traditional switch constructs

At present, the syntax of `switch` statements is highly constrained. It is not as powerful as the `if-else` construct. With `if-else` constructs, you can define and match complex patterns; but not with the `switch` construct. Also, the syntax of `switch` is verbose, which makes it visually annoying. This can lead to error-prone code that can be difficult to debug.

Let's work with an example to show all of these issues. The following example defines an enum, `Size`. The `Shirt` class defines a `setSize()` method, which accepts `Size` and accordingly assigns an integer value to the instance variable, `length`:

```
enum Size {XS, S, M, L, XL, XXL};
class Shirt {
    private int length;
    public void setSize(Size size) {
        switch(size) {
            case XS :   length = 10;
                        System.out.println(length);
                        break;
            case S  :   length = 12;
                        System.out.println(length);
                        break;
            case M  :   length = 14;
                        System.out.println(length);
            case L  :   length = 16;
                        break;
            case XL :   length = 18;
                        System.out.println(length);
                        break;
            case XXL:   length = 20;
                        System.out.println(length);
                        break;
        }
    }
}
```

Here's how you can call the preceding method:

```
Shirt s = new Shirt();
s.setSize(Size.XXL);
System.out.println(s.length);
```

The preceding code outputs the following expected results:

```
20
20
```

However, let's see what happens when you try executing the following code:

```
Shirt s = new Shirt();
s.setSize(Size.M);
System.out.println(s.length);
```

The preceding code outputs an unexpected mismatch in the values:

```
14
16
```

What do you think is the reason for these mismatching values? To answer this question, here's a quick recap—the `switch` branches (that is, the `case` labels) in existing `switch` constructs must include a `break` statement to prevent the fall through of the control. This essentially means that, when the control finds a matching `case` value, it will execute the statements until it finds a `break` statement or it reaches the end of the `switch` construct.

On closer inspection, you'll realize that the branch corresponding to the M value doesn't define a `break` statement. The branch corresponding to the next case, that is, L, misses the `System.out.println` value statement. So, when you call `s.setSize(Size.M)`, the following happens:

1. 14 is assigned to the `length` instance variable
2. `System.out.println()` outputs 14
3. Control falls through the arm corresponding to the L value
4. 16 is assigned to the `length` instance variable

 The traditional `switch` construct has a **default** fall through of control across the `case` labels, in the absence of a `break` statement; this leads to unexpected bugs.

The `switch` construct works as a block. However, if you revisit the example code in the preceding section, you'll agree that the language construct takes the focus away from the business logic and introduces complexity.

This is shown in the following diagram:

What I want 😊	What I get 🙁

① examine variable size
 	
② initialize variable length accordingly
 	
③ Output value of variable length
	`switch (size)){`
	
	        10
	`    case xs:` `length=20;`
	`                System.out.println (length);`
	`                break;`
	`    case  s:` _____
	
	        _____
	        _____

The new `switch` expressions are here to bring the spotlight back to the business logic.

Using switch expressions

Here's an example of a traditional `switch` construct that is modifying a variable based on an enum value passed to a method:

```
enum SingleUsePlastic {STRAW, BAG, SPOON, FORK, KNIFE, PLATE, BOTTLE};

class Planet {
    private static long damage;
    public void use(SingleUsePlastic plastic) {
        switch(plastic) {
            case STRAW :    damage += 10;
                            break;
            case BAG    :   damage += 11;
                            break;
            case SPOON :    damage += 7;
                            break;
            case FORK   :   damage += 7;
                            break;
            case KNIFE :    damage += 7;
                            break;
            case PLATE :    damage += 15;
                            break;
            case BOTTLE:    damage = 20;
                            break;
```

```
            }
         }
      }
```

Let's see how the preceding code changes if we use `switch` expressions:

```
damage += switch(plastic) {
               case STRAW -> 10;
               case BAG -> 11;
               case SPOON, FORK, KNIFE -> 7;
               case PLATE -> 15;
               case BOTTLE -> 20;
         };
```

Let's compare the new `switch` expressions with traditional `switch` statements. The code in the preceding block, which uses `switch` expressions, is a lot more concise. You define what to execute on the right of the arrow (`->`). Also, you no longer need `break` statements in each `switch` branch. There's less boilerplate and less likelihood of accidental errors from missing `break` statements.

The following diagram highlights the changes:

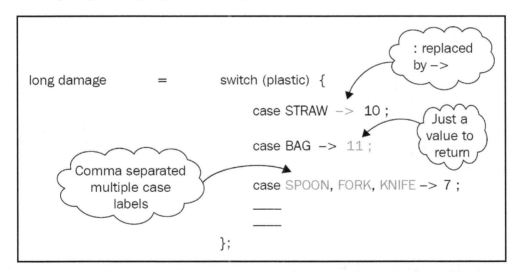

 These `switch` expressions are in addition to traditional `switch` constructs. They are not here to replace existing `switch` constructs.

A `switch` expression offers multiple benefits and features:

- Unlike a `switch` statement, a `switch` expression can return a value
- The return value for a `switch` branch is defined to the right of ->
- The same `switch` branch can define multiple labels that are separated using ,
- There isn't any default fall through of the control across `switch` branches
- The code is less verbose

Let's work with the finer details of `switch` expressions.

Defining local variables in a switch branch

It is possible to define variables that are local to a `switch` branch. To do so, a `switch` branch can define a block of code to execute for a matching `case` label. To return the value from the branch, it can include a `break` statement specifying the value to return.

Let's modify the code in the preceding example to define a code block, as follows:

```
class Planet {
    private static long damage;
    public void use(SingleUsePlastic plastic) {
        damage += switch(plastic) {
            case STRAW -> 10;
            case BAG -> 11;
            case SPOON, FORK, KNIFE -> 7;
            case PLATE -> {
                            int radius = 20;  // Local variable
                            break (radius < 10 ? 15 : 20); // Using
                                            // break to return
                                            // a value

                         }
            case BOTTLE -> 20;
        };
    }
}
```

The scope and accessibility of the local variable, `radius`, are limited to the `switch` branch, in which it is defined.

Another syntax for switch expressions

Apart from using -> to specify the return value, a switch expression can also use a colon (:) to mark the beginning of the code to execute and a break statement to return a value. Here's an example:

```
class Planet {
    private static long damage;
    public void use(SingleUsePlastic plastic) {
        damage += switch(plastic) {
            case STRAW : break 10;       // Use colon (:) to start code,
                                         // Use break to return val
            case BAG   : break 11;
            case SPOON, FORK, KNIFE : break 7;
            case PLATE : int radius = 6;        // no need
                                                // of using curly brace
                      break (radius < 10 ? 15 : 20); // Using
                                                     // break to
                                                     // return a value
            case BOTTLE : break 20;
        };
    }
}
```

Comparing break with break <return value>

A break statement of the break <return value> form is referred to as an **extended break statement**.

A traditional switch construct uses a break statement without any return values in its switch branches, to take control out of a switch construct. This also <indexentry content="break:comparing, with break ">prevents fall through the control <indexentry content="break :comparing, with break">across multiple switch branches. A switch expression uses a break statement with a return value and breaks out of switch expressions.

Let's compare the `break` statement with the `return` statement, which can be used with or without a value. In a method, you can use a `return` statement to return a value and exit a method or just exit a method without returning a value. Here's a quick example:

```
int sum(int x, int y) {                         // return type of method is
                                                // int
    int result = x + y;
    return result;                              // returns int value
}

void output(List<Integer> list) {               // return type of method is
                                                // void
    if (list == null)
        return;                                 // exit method without
                                                // returning a value
    else {
        for (Integer i : list)
            System.out.println(i);
    }
    System.out.println("End of method");  // this doesn't execute if
                                          // list is null
}
```

A `switch` expression uses `break` to return a value. A traditional `switch` construct uses a `break` statement to prevent the fall through of control across its `case` labels.

A preview language feature

A `switch` expression is a preview language feature (JEP 12). This essentially means that, even though it is complete, it has a possibility of not being confirmed as a permanent feature in a future Java release. This happens for a reason.

Java runs on billions of devices and is used by millions of developers. The risks are high for any mistake in a new Java language feature. Before permanently adding a language feature to Java, the architects of Java evaluate what the developers have to say about it—that is, how good or bad it is. Depending on the feedback, a preview language feature might be refined before it's added to Java SE or dropped completely. So, if you have any feedback on `switch` expressions, please share it with `amber-dev` (`https://mail.openjdk.java.net/mailman/listinfo/amber-dev`).

Exhaustive cases

A `switch` expression can be used to return a value or just execute a set of statements, like the traditional `switch` statement.

When you are using a `switch` expression to return a value that is used to assign a value to a variable, its cases must be exhaustive. This essentially means that, whatever value you pass to the `switch` argument, it must be able to find an appropriate branch to execute. A `switch` expression can accept arguments of the `byte`, `short`, `int`, `Byte`, `Short`, `Integer`, or `String` types or enums. Of these, only an enum has exhaustive values.

In the following example, a `switch` expression is being used to assign a value to the `damage` variable. Since there is no matching branch to execute for the `PLATE` value, this code won't compile:

```
class Planet {
    private static long damage;
    public void use(SingleUsePlastic plastic) {
        damage += switch(plastic) {
            case SPOON, FORK, KNIFE -> 7;
        };
    }
}
```

To compile the preceding code, you can either add the `switch` branch with the `case` label, `PLATE`, or add a `default` branch, as follows:

```
class Planet {
    private static long damage;
    public void use(SingleUsePlastic plastic) {
        damage += switch(plastic) {
            case SPOON, FORK, KNIFE -> 7;
            // Adding (1) or (2), or both will enable the code to
            // compile
            case PLATE -> 10;      // line number (1)
            default -> 100;        // line number (2)
        };
    }
}
```

For `switch` arguments such as primitive types, wrapper classes, or `String` classes, which don't have an exhaustive list of values, you must define a default `case` label (if you are returning a value from `switch` expressions), as follows:

```
String getBook(String name) {
    String bookName = switch(name) {
        case "Shreya" -> "Harry Potter";
        case "Paul" -> "Management tips";
        case "Harry" -> "Life of Pi";
        default -> "Design Patters - everyone needs this";
    };
    return bookName;
}
```

Let's work with the second situation where you are *not* using `switch` expressions to return a value. The following code modifies the `getBook()` method from the preceding code. Though `switch` expressions use the new syntax (using -> to define the code to execute), it is *not* returning a value. In such a case, the cases of a `switch` expression need *not* be exhaustive:

```
String getBook(String name) {
    String bookName = null;
    switch(name) {                                        // NOT returning
                                                          // a value
        case "Shreya" -> bookName = "Harry Potter";
        case "Paul" -> bookName = "Management tips";
        case "Harry" -> bookName = "Life of Pi";      // default case
                                                      // not included
    }
    return bookName;
}
```

 When you use `switch` expressions to return a value, its cases must be exhaustive, otherwise, your code won't compile. When you are using `switch` expressions to execute a set of statements without returning a value, it's cases might not be exhaustive.

What can a switch branch execute other than returning a value?

In a `switch` expression, when a `switch` branch isn't returning a value, it can execute a single statement, a block of statements, or even throw an exception. In the following example, the `switch` statement is not returning a value. It executes a single statement (prints out a value) for the `case` label, `Sun`; executes a block of code for the `case` labels, `Mon` and `Tue`; and throws an exception for its default case:

```
String day = // assign a value here
switch(day) {
    case "Sun" -> System.out.println("OSS-Jav");
    case "Mon", "Tue" -> {
        // some simple/complex code
    }
    default -> throw new RuntimeException("Running out of projects");
}
```

How not to use labels and continue in switch expressions

You can use labels and a `continue` statement within `switch` expressions. However, you can't jump through `switch` expressions by using them as follows. Here's an example:

```
class Planet {
    private static long damage;
    public void use(SingleUsePlastic plastic) {
        myLabel:                                        // Label
            for (...) {
                damage += switch(plastic) {
                    case SPOON, FORK, KNIFE : break 7;
                    case PLATE : continue myLabel;      // NOT
                                                        // allowed
                                                        // illegal
                                                        // jump
                                                        // through
                                                        // switch
                                                        // expression
                };
            }
    }
}
```

Summary

In this chapter, you saw how `switch` expressions have enhanced the traditional `switch` statement. You can use `switch` expressions to return a value that can be used to initialize variables or reassign values to them. It also makes your code less verbose. By removing default fall through of the control across `switch` branches, you are less likely to introduce logical errors with `switch` expressions.

In the next chapter, we'll cover multiple improvements and additions in JDK 12.

12
Miscellaneous Improvements in JDK 12

Java 12 is the latest **Short Term Support** (**STS**) release by Oracle. However, the industry is still warming to migrating to the latest **Long-Term-Support** (**LTS**) Java release by Oracle, that is, Java 11.

The notable features in JDK 12 are the addition of Shenandoah GC and `switch` expressions. We covered `switch` expressions in `Chapter 11`, *Switch Expressions*. Since a detailed coverage of Shenandoah GC is beyond the scope of this book, I'm covering it in this chapter with the remaining additions and updates to Java 12.

In this chapter, we'll cover the following topics:

- Shenandoah—a low-pause-time GC
- The microbenchmark suite
- The **Java Virtual Machine** (**JVM**) Constants API
- One AArch64 port, not two
- Default CDS archives
- Abortable mixed collections for G1
- Promptly return unused committed memory from G1

Technical requirements

To use the features that are included in this chapter, you should have JDK 12 or a later version on your system.

Since this chapter covers multiple features in Java 12, let's quickly map the features with their **JDK Enhancement Proposal** (**JEP**) number and scope.

Mapping features of JDK 12 scope and JEP

The following table lists the JDK 12 features covered in this chapter, their corresponding JEP number, and their scope:

JEP	Scope	Description
189	Implementation	Shenandoah—a low-pause-time GC
230	JDK	The microbenchmark suite
334	SE	The JVM constants API
340	JDK	One AArch64 port, not two
341	JDK	Default CDS archives
344	Implementation	Abortable mixed collections for G1
346	Implementation	Promptly return unused committed memory from G1

Let's get started with the first feature.

Shenandoah – a low-pause-time GC

Proposed and developed by engineers at Red Hat, Shenandoah GC promises significantly low pauses. It is a region-based GC that collects garbage in a parallel and concurrent manner. It is interesting to note that the pause times are independent of the application's live data.

With hardware engineering and lower costs, servers have more memory and processing power than ever before. Modern applications are increasingly demanding lower pause times—with **Service Level Agreement** (**SLA**) applications that guarantee response times of 10 to 500 ms. To meet the lower end of this range, a GC should be able to accomplish multiple tasks, including the following:

- Use algorithms that enable programs to execute with the given memory
- Keep the pause times low (that is, below 10 ms)

Is this attainable with, say, a Java application that uses 200 GB memory? This isn't possible with the compacting algorithms, which will exceed the limit of 10 ms, even for compacting 10% of this memory. Shenandoah uses an algorithm that compacts the memory concurrently while the Java threads are running. In this case, objects are moved during a concurrent GC cycle and all of its references immediately access the newer copy.

Concurrent compaction isn't simple. When GC moves a live object, it must **atomically** update all references to the object, pointing to the new object. However, to find all of the references, the entire heap should be scanned; this sounds infeasible. To get around this, the Shenandoah GC adds a **forwarding pointer** to each object, with each use of that object going through that pointer. This simplifies the process of moving around objects. The Shenandoah GC thread or application thread can copy an object and use compare and swap to update the forwarding pointer. In case of contention, only one compare and swap will succeed. With the addition of the forwarding pointer, Shenandoah GC uses more space than other GC algorithms.

Each Shenandoah GC cycle consists of four phases. A Shenandoah GC cycle begins with **Initial Marking**, in which it *stops the world* and scans the root set. In phase two, that is, **Concurrent Marking**, it marks the live objects and updates references, concurrently. In the third phase, **Final Marking**, it *stops the world* and scans the root set again, copying and updating roots to updated copies. The last phase, **Concurrent Compaction**, evacuates live objects from the targeted regions.

Shenandoah is a region-based GC. It isn't a generational GC that focuses on collecting the youngest objects. This is based on the hypothesis that most objects die young. However, applications with caches hold on to the objects long enough, and so generational GC algorithms don't work with them. To get around this, Shenandoah uses the **Least Recently Used (LRU)** cache benchmark that enables it to keep its pause time low.

Shenandoah never compacts humongous objects (that is, objects that can't fit in one region and require multiple regions). If the Shenandoah GC cycle determines that a humongous object is no longer live, its region is immediately reclaimed.

The main target of Shenandoah GC is to increase the responsiveness of the JVM by lowering the count and duration of GC cycles.

The microbenchmark suite

Based on **Java Microbenchmark Harness (JMH)**, this feature adds a basic suite of microbenchmarks to the JDK source code, with the following proposed directory structure:

```
jdk/jdk
    .../make/test
    .../test
        .../micro/org/openjdk/bench
            .../java
                .../vm
```

Since the microbenchmark suite will be located with the JDK source code, it will make it simpler for developers to locate and run existing microbenchmarks, and create new ones. As existing features are updated or removed from a JDK version, it will be simple to update a microbenchmark. Also, when developers run a microbenchmark they can use JMH's powerful filtering to run selected benchmarks.

Although the microbenchmark suite and its building will be integrated with JDK and its build system, it will have a separate target. Developers will need to specify additional parameters to execute it to keep the build time for normal JDK low.

As the name suggests, with benchmarking you can compare builds or releases. Hence, the microbenchmarks support JDK (*N*) for the new JDK and JDK (*N-1*) for the previous release. The benchmarks depend on JMH in the same way that unit tests depend on TestNG or `jtreg`. JMH is used during the build process and is packaged as part of the resulting JAR file.

The JVM constants API

This JEP introduces an API to standardize the description and loading of class constants.

Every Java class has a constant pool. It either stores simple values such as strings and integers or values to represent classes or methods. Class constant pool values are used as operand values for the **ldc (load constant)** bytecode instruction. These constants can also be used by the **invokedynamic** bytecode instruction—in the static argument list of a bootstrap method.

When either an ldc or invokedynamic instruction executes, it represents the constant value as a Java data type value, a class, an integer, or a string. Until now, the responsibility of modeling bytecode instructions and loading constants was on the class that wanted to manipulate class files. This usually takes the focus of these classes off their business logic, moving it to the specifics of how to model bytecode instructions and load class constants. This is clearly a good candidate to separate the concerns and define the API to work with the *how* part.

Also, it isn't easy for classes to implement this functionality by themselves, because loading class constants isn't a simple process for non-string and non-integer values. Class loading is a complex process and has multiple points of failure. Class loading is dependent on the host environment, including the existence of classes, the ability to gain access to them, and their relevant permissions. Class loading could also fail during the linking process.

An absence of a standardized library to handle these functions of loading constants also results in mismatched expectations between programs.

JDK 12 defines a new package, `java.lang.invoke.constant`, which defines a family of value-based symbolic reference types. It can be used to describe all types of loadable constants. A symbolic constant uses a nominal form and essentially excludes a constant from its loading or accessibility context. The package includes types such as `ClassDesc`, `MethodTypeDesc`, `MethodHandleDesc`, and `DynamicConstantDes` to describe various constants. Data types such as `String`, `Integer`, `Long`, `Float`, and `Double` are also used to represent simple class constants.

There are varied use cases of this package. Libraries that parse or generate bytecodes need to describe classes and method handles in a symbolic manner. Bootstraps for invokedynamic will get simpler because they will be able to work with symbolic representation, rather than working with live classes and method handles. It will be simpler for the compiler and offline transformers to describe classes and their members, which can't be loaded into the running **Virtual Machine** (**VM**). Compiler plugins, such as annotation processors, also need to describe uses classes and their members in symbolic terms.

One AArch64 port, not two

Until version 12, JDK had two 64-bit ARM ports, even though both produce an AArch64 implementation. As a maintenance feature, this JEP removes all sources related to the 64-bit 64-bit ARM platform and retains the 64-bit ARM AArch64 port. It will prevent the duplication of work to maintain two ports. As part of the process, the option to build this port will also be removed from JDK. It will also validate that the 32-bit ARM port continues to work as expected and that it isn't affected by these changes.

Default CDS archives

To understand the enhancements to CDS archives with JDK 12, let's quickly recap what CDS is and how it impacts your applications. I covered this briefly in `Chapter 2`, *AppCDS*.

What is CDS?

A commercial feature with Oracle JVM since Java 8, CDS helps to reduce the start up time of a Java application and its memory footprint. This is especially notable when you are working with multiple JVMs.

On startup, JVM prepares the environment for execution. It includes bytecode loading, verification, linking, and initializing of the core classes and interfaces. The classes and interfaces are combed into the runtime state of the JVM so that they can be executed. It also includes method areas and constant pools.

These set of core classes and interfaces don't change unless you update your JVM. So, every time you start your JVM, it performs the *same* steps to get the environment up for execution. Imagine that you could dump the result to a file, which could be read by your JVM at startup. The subsequent startups could get the environment up and running without performing the intermediate steps of loading, verification, linking, and initialization; welcome to CDS.

When you install JRE, CDS creates a shared archive file from a predefined set of classes from the system JAR file. Classes are verified by the class loaders before they can be used and this process applies to all of the classes. To speed up this process, the installation process loads these classes into an internal representation and then dumps that representation to `classes.jsa`—the shared archive file. When the JVM starts or restarts, the shared archive file is memory mapped to save the loading of those classes.

When the JVM's metadata is shared among multiple JVM processes, it results in a smaller memory footprint. Loading classes from a populated cache are faster than loading them from the disk; they are also partially verified. This feature is also beneficial for Java applications that start new JVM instances.

Using CDS archives have reportedly resulted in the reduction of the application start up time by more than 30% on basic programs such as `HelloWorld` with JDK 11. This number is even higher on numerous 64-bit platforms.

Enhancing CDS

Often, developers end up not using a feature that could enhance the performance of their application—out of ignorance—by just missing a step. Or should we call it a usability issue?

At present, even though the JDK includes a default class list, it can be used with the following command:

```
java -Xshare:dump
```

Even though this behavior is documented, developers miss reading the document, and hence, can't use this feature.

JDK 12 modifies the build process. It runs the `java -Xshare:dump` command after linking it to the class list. To ensure that the CDS archive file is part of the JDK image, the shared archive file is placed in the `lib/server` directory.

The shared archive file is used **automatically** during application startup, since `-Xshare:auto` is the default option with the server VM in JDK 11. So, unless it is specifically turned off using the `-Xshare:off` option, developers and applications will continue using it without executing any additional commands or set up.

CDS includes a predefined list of classes and interfaces from the core Java API. For the inclusion of specific API or application classes, or for specific GC behavior, developers can create and use a custom archive file.

Abortable mixed collections for G1

Developers are increasingly demanding more definite behavior from GCs. For instance, wouldn't you prefer to execute your application with a GC that guarantees an upper limit to its pause timings?

When working with G1 GC in Java 12, you can abort *mixed collections* if they exceed your specified limit. Note that you can't abort *all* categories of G1 GC pauses.

A mixed collection includes both *young* and *old* memory regions for G1 to clean. An analysis system selects the set of regions, collectively called a **collection set**, for G1 GC to work on. Prior to JDK 12, G1 GC could exceed the maximum pause time when the collection set was too large, the collection set included too many old regions, or the collection set included regions with *stale* data.

With JDK 12, when G1 collects live objects from mixed collections, it can do so in an incremental manner, so that it doesn't exceed the maximum pause timings. This process splits the collection set into mandatory and optional parts. After G1 completes collecting live objects from the mandatory collection, it collects objects from the optional set, if time permits.

Promptly return unused committed memory from G1

An additional enhancement to G1 GC—to return the Java heap memory to the **Operating System (OS)** when idle. This enhancement is most likely to be triggered by the increase in container environments that are used to run applications on the JVM.

Prior to Java 12, G1 returned memory from the Java heap in two cases—while performing a full GC or during a concurrent cycle. However, neither of these instances happen very often. In fact, G1 performs a full GC as its last resort to free up memory. A concurrent cycle is subjected to the Java heap allocation and occupancy.

This GC behavior has multiple disadvantages—organizations pay more for the memory even though it isn't used in an efficient manner in container environments, and service providers under-utilize their resources. In this enhancement, the JVM determines the *idle* times for an application and returns the memory to the OS. This makes a lot of sense since the usage of applications isn't the same across the days of the week or even hours of a day. This enhancement can save organizations a lot of money when deploying their application to environments that provide resources as a service.

Summary

In this chapter, we browsed through the various additions and modifications to JDK 12, barring one of its preview language features of `switch` expressions.

The features covered in this chapter were mostly related to the JDK and its implementation. We covered one of the newest additions to the growing GC family—Shenandoah. A concurrent GC, Shenandoah promises ultra-low pause times for modern Java applications, irrespective of their memory sizes. The other two GC features mentioned—abortable mixed collections for G1 and promptly return unused committed memory from G1—also enhance the existing G1 GC.

The JVM constants API introduces a new package and classes to represent class constraints symbolically. Apart from easing its usage across libraries and classes, the JVM constant API will standardize the constants. Default CDS archives improve the process of the creation of archive files. The removal of the source for an AArch64 ARM port is more related to housekeeping.

In the next chapter, we will look into the details and features of Project Amber.

Section 4: Project Amber

In this section, you will first be introduced to enums, which enable you to define a new type. Then, we will learn more about the data classes in Project Amber and cover the challenges of using POJOs to model data. Following on from this, you'll learn more about an exciting language enhancement—raw string literals. Next, we will see what Java has in the pipeline in terms of helping to overcome problems related to lambdas and method references, before ending with pattern matching, which will include the addition of new capabilities to Java.

The following chapters will be covered in this section:

- Chapter 13, *Enhanced Enums in Project Amber*
- Chapter 14, *Data Classes and Their Usage*
- Chapter 15, *Raw String Literals*
- Chapter 16, *Lambda Leftovers*
- Chapter 17, *Pattern Matching*

13
Enhanced Enums in Project Amber

Enums add type safety to finite and predefined sets of constants. Enums enable you to define a new type (such as a class or an interface) with a state and behavior. **Project Amber** is enhancing enums, taking them to the next level by adding type variables (generics) and allowing sharper enum type-checking. These will enable enums to define constants with type information, state, and behavior—applicable exclusively to each constant. These enhancements will reduce the need to refactor enums to classes in order to use generics.

In this chapter, we'll cover the following topics:

- The reason for enhancing enums
- Adding a state and behavior to enum constants
- Creating generic enums
- Accessing a constant, specific state and behavior
- Performing sharper type-checking for enum constants

A quick background

Enums introduced type safety to the use of constants, which were defined previously by using `static`, and `final` variables of a type such as `int`.

An example

Imagine limiting the sizes of a shirt to some predefined sizes (such as `Small`, `Medium`, and `Large`). The following code shows how you can do that with an enum (`Size`):

```
enum Size {SMALL, MEDIUM, LARGE}
```

Java's coding guidelines recommend using uppercase to define enum constants (such as `SMALL`). Multiple words in a constant can be separated by using an underscore.

The following code shows how you can use the `Size` enum in a class, `Shirt`, to restrict its sizes to constants defined in the `Size` enum:

```
class Shirt {
    Size size;                   // instance variable of type Size
    Color color;

    Shirt(Size size, Color color) {     // Size object with Shirt
                                         // instantiation

        this.size = size;
        this.color = color;
    }
}
```

The instance variable of the `Size` type in the `Shirt` class limits the values that are assigned to it to `Size.SMALL`, `Size.MEDIUM`, and `Size.LARGE`. The following code is an example of how another class, `GarmentFactory`, uses enum constants to create instances of the `Shirt` class:

```
class GarmentFactory {
    void createShirts() {
        Shirt redShirtS = new Shirt(Size.SMALL, Color.red);
        Shirt greenShirtM = new Shirt(Size.MEDIUM, Color.green);
        Shirt redShirtL = new Shirt(Size.LARGE, Color.red);
    }
}
```

 Enums define new types with predefined sets of constant values. Enums add type safety to constant values.

Decompiled enum – behind the scenes

Every user-defined enum implicitly extends the `java.lang.Enum` class. Behind the scenes, the one-line `Size` enum (defined in the preceding section) is compiled into something similar to the following (I've added comments in the code to explain it; when you compile an enum, you won't get similar comments):

```
final class Size extends Enum            // 'enum' converted to final
class
{
    public static final Size SMALL;      // variables to store
    public static final Size MEDIUM;     // enum constants
    public static final Size LARGE;      //

    private static final Size $VALUES[];  // array of all enum
                                          // constants


    static
    {                                    // static initializer
        SMALL = new Size("SMALL", 0);    // to initialize enum
                                         // constants
        MEDIUM = new Size("MEDIUM", 1);  //
        LARGE = new Size("LARGE", 2);    //
        $VALUES = (new Size[] {          //
            SMALL, MEDIUM, LARGE         // & populate array of enum
                                         // constants
        });
    }
    public static Size[] values()
    {
            return (Size[])$VALUES.clone();      // Avoiding any
                                                 // modification to
    }                                   // $VALUES by calling methods
    public static Size valueOf(String s)
    {
        return (Size)Enum.valueOf(Size, s);
    }
    private Size(String s, int i)
    {
        super(s, i);
    }
}
```

 Enums are syntactic sugar. The compiler takes your enum construct and extends java.lang.Enum to create a class. It adds the variables, initializers, and methods to get the required behavior.

The state and behavior of enum constants

The enum constants can have their own states and behaviors. You can define a state and behavior that is common to all enum constants, or states and behaviors that are specific to each one of them. But can you access them later? Let's find out.

Adding states and behaviors to enum constants

You can add states and behaviors to enum constants by defining instance variables and methods in an enum. All of these are accessible by the enum constants. Let's modify the `Size` enum defined in the previous section, by adding a state and behavior to it. Each enum constant can define a constant, specific class body, define a new state and behavior, or override the default behavior of the enum methods in which it is defined. The following is an example of this:

```
enum Size {
    SMALL(36, 19),
    MEDIUM(32, 20) {                         // Constant specific class body
        int number = 10;                     // variable specific to
                                             //MEDIUM
        int getSize() {                      // method specific to
                                             //MEDIUM
            return length + width;
        }
    },
    LARGE(34, 22) {
        @Override
        public String toText() {             // overriding method toText
                                             //for
            return "LARGE";                  // constant LARGE
        }
    };

    int length;                              // instance variable
                                             //accessible
    int width;                               // to all enum constants

    Size(int length, int width) {            // enum constructor;
                                             //accepts length
        this.length = length;                // and width
        this.width = width;
    }

    int getLength() {                        // method accessible to all
                                             //enum
```

```
        return length;                          // constants
    }

    int getWidth() {                            // method accessible to all
                                                //enum
        return width;                           // constants
    }

    public String toText() {                    // method accessible to all
                                                //enum
        return length + " X " + width;          // constants
    }
}
```

In the preceding example, the Size enum defines three enum constants—SMALL, MEDIUM, and LARGE. It also defines instance variables (length and breadth), a constructor, and the getLength(), getWidth, and toText() methods.

Accessing the state and behavior of enum constants

At present, an enum constant can access the following:

- The state and behavior common to all enum constants
- Overridden methods

For the Size enum (defined in the preceding section), you can access the state and behavior common to all enum constants, as follows:

```
System.out.println(Size.SMALL.toText());   // toString is defined for all
constants
```

The preceding code will have the following output:

36 X 19

You can also access the behavior that a specific enum constant overrides as follows:

```
System.out.println(Size.LARGE.toText());
```

The preceding code will have the following output:

LARGE

However, you can't access the state or behavior that is specific to an enum constant, as shown in the following code:

```
System.out.println(Size.MEDIUM.number);        // Doesn't compile
System.out.println(Size.MEDIUM.getSize());     // Doesn't compile
```

The `getSize()` method and the `number` variable can't be accessed by using the `MEDIUM` constant. That is because `MEDIUM` creates an anonymous class and overrides the methods of the `Size` enum. It can't access the constant, specific state or behavior, because it's still referenced by a variable of the `Size` type. The following figure should help you remember this:

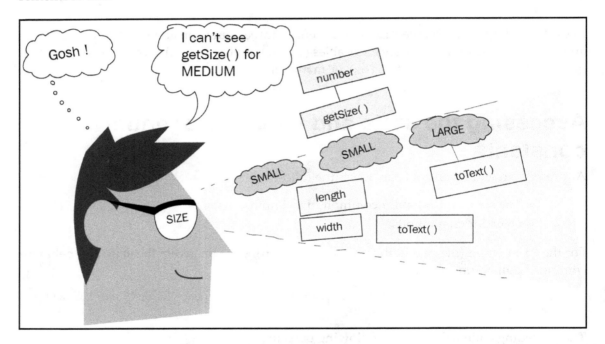

Existing enums don't allow access to a state or behavior that is specific to an enum constant, because it creates an anonymous class to do so.

Workarounds to access enum constants

One of the ways to access members such as variables and methods that are specific to an enum constant is—to define them for all members, but only allow the usage for specific members (I know, this is not recommended). I've removed code that is not relevant to show how this works, as follows:

```
enum Size {
    SMALL(36, 19),
    MEDIUM(32, 20),
    LARGE(34, 22);
    int length;                              // instance variable
                                             //accessible
    int width;                               // to all enum constants
    Size(int length, int width) {            // enum constructor; accepts
                                             //length
        this.length = length;                // and width
        this.width = width;
    }
    int getSize() {
        if (this == MEDIUM)
            return length + width;
        else                                 // throws runtime
                                             // exception
            throw new UnsupportedOperationException();  // if used with
                                             // constants
    }                                        // other than
                                             //MEDIUM
}
```

Let's try to access the method `getSize()` using enum constants:

```
System.out.println(MEDIUM.getSize());
System.out.println(LARGE.getSize());
```

The output of the preceding code is as follows:

52
Exception in thread—java.lang.UnsupportedOperationException

First and foremost, adding code (the `getSize()` method) that is not applicable to all enum constants breaks the encapsulation. In the preceding example, I defined `getSize()` in the main body, whereas only the `MEDIUM` enum constant required the `getSize()` method. This is neither desirable nor recommended.

Compared it with an arrangement of a base class and its derived classes, adding all of the behaviors specific to the different derived classes in your base class. However, it's not recommended as it doesn't define the encapsulated code.

Using inheritance with enum constants

The following is another example of an enum, that works with a set of subclasses by passing instances of subclasses to the enum constructor. To get the point across, I've modified the `Size` enum, which we have been working on with since the beginning of this chapter. The following is the modified code:

```java
class Measurement {}                    // base class
class Small extends Measurement {       // derived class
    String text = "Small";              // state specific to class
                                        //Small
}
class Medium extends Measurement {      // derived class
    public int getLength() {            // behavior specific to class
                                        //Medium
        return 9999;
    }
}
class Large extends Measurement {}      // derived class

enum Size {
    SMALL(new Small()),                 // constant created using Small
                                        //instance
    MEDIUM(new Medium()),               // constant created using Medium
                                        //instance
    LARGE(new Large());                 // constant created using Large
                                        //instance

    private Measurement mObj;           // Measurement is base class of
                                        // classes Small, Medium & Large

    Size(Measurement obj) {             // wraps Measurement instance as an
                                        //Enum instance
        mObj = obj;
    }
    Measurement getMeasurement() { // get the wrapped instance
        return mObj;
    }
}
```

Again, you can't access the state and behavior of the enum-constant-specific code. The following is an example:

```
class Test1 {
    public static void main(String args[]) {
        var large = Size.LARGE;
        System.out.println(large.getMeasurement()
                            .getLength());      // doesn't compile
                                                // the type of the
                                                // variable used
                                                // to wrap the value
                                                // of enum
                                                // constant is
                                                // Measurement
    }
}
```

Here, the enhanced enums come to the rescue. JEP 301 introduced enhanced enums by adding type variables or generics to it. Let's look at how it works in the next section.

Adding generics to enums

Let's rewrite the enum code from the preceding example, adding a variable type to the enum `Size`. The bounded type parameter (`<T extends Measurement>`) restricts the types that can be passed as arguments to the `Size` enum, to the `Measurement` class and its derived classes.

 This section modifies the code from the preceding section. To understand the example code and its purpose, please read the preceding section (if you haven't already).

The modified code is as follows:

```
enum Size <T extends Measurement> {        // enum with type parameter
    SMALL(new Small()),
    MEDIUM(new Medium()),
    LARGE(new Large());

    private T mObj;

    Size(T obj) {
        mObj = obj;
    }
    T getMeasurement() {
```

```
            return mObj;
        }
    }

class Measurement {}
class Small extends Measurement {
    String text = "Small";
}
class Medium extends Measurement {}
class Large extends Measurement {
    public int getLength() {
        return 40;
    }
}
```

The following code can be used to access behavior that is specific to a constant, say, the getLength() method, which is accessible only to the LARGE constant, as follows:

```
var large = Size.LARGE;
System.out.println(large.getMeasurement().getLength());
```

 With the enhanced enums (with generics added), you will be able to access an enum constant specific state or behavior.

Let's work with another example of a generic enum, which can be used to restrict the user data to certain types.

The following example creates a generic enum, Data, which can be passed as a type parameter, T:

```
public enum Data<T> {
    NAME<String>,          // constants of generic
    AGE<Integer>,          // enum Data
    ADDRESS<Address>;
}
```

The FormData class defines a generic method that can accept a constant of the Data enum and a value of the same type that is used for the enum constant:

```
public class FormData {
    public <T> void add(Data<T> type, T value) {
        //..code
    }
}
```

The following code shows how you can use the constants of the `Data` enum to restrict the combination of types of values that you pass to the `add` method:

```
FormData data = new FormData();
data.add(Data.NAME, "Pavni");         // okay; type of NAME and
                                      // Pavni is String
data.add(Data.AGE, 22);               // okay; type of AGE and 22 is
                                      // Integer
data.add(Data.ADDRESS, "California"); // Won't compile. "California"
                                      // is String, not Address
                                      // instance
```

With the mismatched data, the code fails at compilation, making it easier for the developer to correct it.

> Compilation failures are always better than runtime exceptions. Using the generic `Data` enum will make the code fail at compile time for a mismatched combination of values passed to `add()`.

Sharper typing of enum constants

One of the two major goals of enhanced enums is to perform sharper type-checking for enums. At present, the type of all enum constants is the enum in which they are defined. Referring to our example enum, `Size`, this essentially means that the type of all of the enum constants (`SMALL`, `MEDIUM`, and `LARGE`) is `Size`, which is incorrect (as depicted in the following figure):

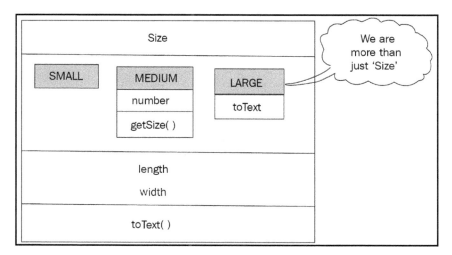

Although enum constants are allowed to define a constant specific class body, which includes variables and methods, the constant type is not sharp enough to allow for access to enum constant-specific values. Even in the case of generic enums, the static type of an enum constant is not sharp enough to capture the full type information of individual constants.

Summary

In this chapter, you learned about how the enums in Java 5 introduced type safety to constants. We covered how each enum constant can have its own distinct state and behavior, not just what is common to all enum constants. However, it's not feasible to access the state and behavior that is specific to an enum constant with the existing enums.

Next, we covered how the enhanced enums can use generics and access a constant specific state and behavior. With examples, we also covered how type parameters facilitate sharper typing of enum constants.

In the next chapter, we'll cover how the data classes in Project Amber are bringing about language changes to define data carrier classes.

Data Classes and Their Usage

14

Concerning the data classes in Project Amber, work is in progress. It proposes to provide developers with a simplified method for modeling data, introducing special classes with the `record` keyword. The state of a data class could be captured by using the class header, which is in stark contrast to the existing **Plain Old Java Objects** (**POJOs**).

In this chapter, we'll cover the following topics:

- An introduction to data classes
- The need for data classes, and their limitations
- The aggregate and exploded forms of data classes
- Pattern matching with data classes
- Inheritance with abstract data classes and interfaces
- Adding variables and methods
- Overriding default behaviors

An introduction to data classes

We know of two versions of data classes—POJO (the old, existing form) and the newly proposed data classes. To understand the data classes that are being worked on in Project Amber, you'll need to know the capabilities and limitations of the existing POJO classes and why we need the newly proposed classes.

 POJO is not implemented using a language construct. The proposed data classes would include changes or additions to the programming language.

What is a data class?

As a Java developer, you have probably used and created POJOs in some (or all) of your projects. A POJO is a class that encapsulates a set of data, without any additional behavior to manipulate its state. It usually includes constructors, accessors, mutators, and the overridden methods from the object class (`hashCode()`, `equals()`, and `toString()`). The accessors and mutators allow access and assignment to state variables. Additionally, the mutators might include code to check the range of values that are assigned to the instance state. The following is an example:

```java
final class Emp {
    private String name;
    private int age;

    public Emp(String name, int age) {
        this.name = name;
        this.age = age;
    }

    // accessor methods - getName, getAge
    public String getName() {
        return name;
    }

    public int getAge() {
        return age;
    }

    // mutator methods - setName, setAge
    public void setName() {
        this.name = name;
    }

    public void setAge() {
        this.age = age;
    }

    public boolean equals(Object obj) {
        if (obj == null || (!(obj instanceof Emp)))
            return false;
        else {
            if ( ( ((Emp)obj).getName().equals(this.name) &&
                ( ((Emp)obj).getAge() ) == this.age)) {
                return true;
            }
            else
                return false;
```

```
        }
    }

    public String toString() {
        return name + ":" + age;
    }
    public int hashCode() {
        // ..code
    }
}
```

One scenario is using the Emp class to save employee data to your database. Here's an example:

```
interface EmpDAO {
    Emp read();
    void write(Emp emp);
    List<Emp> getAllEmp();
}
```

Similarly, you can use the Emp class to be passed in a message, sent over the network, inserted into a JSON object, and more.

All of this looks good. Most importantly, it has been working fine since Java was introduced to developers. So, what is the problem?

The need to add data classes to the language

Imagine securing the borders of a country, which are normally guarded by defense forces. Will the level of security change based on the relationships with the neighboring countries (cordial, neutral, or tense)? What happens if the borders are porous (for example, the borders in Western Europe, for the Schengen countries)? Now, compare guarding the borders of a country with guarding our homes or securing the contents of a cabinet in a room.

Although each instance in the preceding example concerns the security of an entity and its protection from a physical attack, the instances have varying requirements.

Similarly, until now, the classes in Java have been used to model a wide range of requirements. While this works well for a lot of cases, it doesn't work for some. If you want to make the same size fit all, you'll need a lot of adjustments, for most of them.

Compare this to using the same trouser size for individuals with varying heights and waist sizes, as shown in the following diagram:

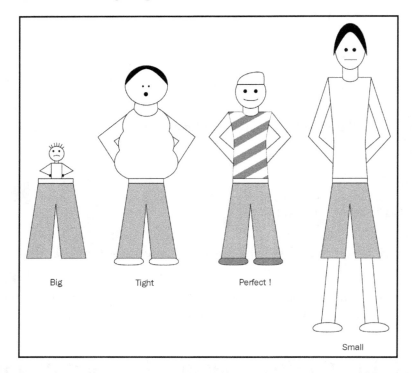

In the past, enums were added to the Java language (version 5). Even though a class can be programmed to create an enumeration of primitives or objects, enums simplified the process for a developer.

 Enums reduced the coding for developers. At the same time, they made the intent of each enum explicit to the users.

In the preceding section, the Emp POJO is just a carrier of its data. However, seasoning a class to behave like a data class requires a developer to define multiple methods—constructs, accessors, mutators, and other methods from the object class. You might argue that you can use an IDE to easily generate all of these methods for your class. You are right! And it's quite simple to do so.

However, that only takes care of the writing part of the code. What happens to the reading part of the code, for the users of the class? Us developers understand that a piece of code might be written just once, but will be read multiple times. That is why experienced programmers stress good coding practices, for comprehending, reading, and maintaining code.

When the definition of data classes is induced in the language, the readers of the code will know its explicit intent of being a data class. The developers need not dig their claws deep into finding the code that was in addition to being a data class, so that they don't miss any important information.

This will also prevent the developers from using half-baked classes as data classes. At times, developers use such classes as a data class, which do not include all of the relevant methods (such as equals() or hashCode()). This will surely lead to inserting subtle bugs in your applications. A collection class, such as Map, requires a class to implement its equals() and hashCode() methods to function properly and efficiently.

Introducing data classes with a change in the language would decrease the verbosity of the language, broadcasting the intent of the structure to all.

Diving into data classes

The syntax to define a data class looks simple. However, both the syntax and semantics are important. Let's get started by looking at some examples, in the following sections.

Example of syntax and semantics

Let's redefine the Emp class, which we used at the beginning of the chapter, as a data class:

```
record Emp(String name, int age) { }     // data class - one liner
                                          // code
```

The preceding code uses the `record` keyword to define a data class, accepting a comma-separated variable `name` and type, required to store the state. The compiler automatically generates default implements for the object methods (`equals()`, `hashCode()`, and `toString()`) for data classes.

The code looks clear and compact. A reader would immediately know the intent of this single line of code—a carrier of the data `name` (type `String`) and `age` (type `int`). Another advantage for a reader is that they wouldn't have to read through constructors, accessors, mutators, or methods of the object class, just to ascertain that they are doing what they are supposed to.

Behind the scenes, the record class, `Emp`, is converted to the following code by the Java compiler:

```
final class Emp extends java.lang.DataClass {
    final String name; final int age;
        public Emp(String name, int age) {
        this.name = name; this.age = age; } // deconstructor // public
        // accessor methods // default implementation of equals,
    // hashCode, and toString }
```

The preceding data class is an example of a non-abstract data class. A data class can also be defined as an abstract data class. A non-abstract data class is implicitly final. In both cases, a data class will get default implementations of `hashCode()`, `equals()`, and `toString()`, and accessor methods. For an abstract data class, the constructors would be protected.

In the following diagram, the compiler looks happy to convert the one line code for the data class to a full-fledged class:

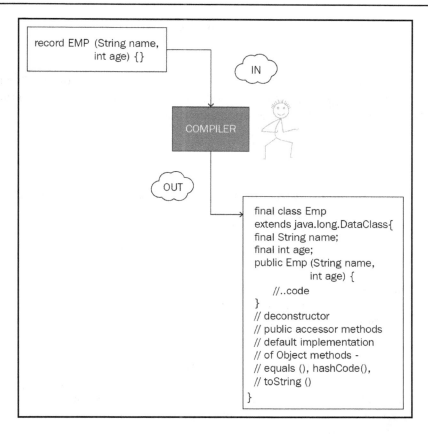

 By default, a data class is `final`; you can't extend it.

The aggregate and exploded forms of data classes

The aggregate form of a data class will be the name of the data class. Its exploded form would refer to the variables used to store its data. The conversion from aggregate to exploded form is referred to as the **deconstruction pattern**.

The following code refers to the example that we used in the preceding section:

```
record Emp(String name, int age) { }
```

Emp is the aggregate form of the Emp data class. Its exploded form would be String name and int age. The language would need easy conversion between the two, so that they can be used with other language constructs, such as switch.

Limitations

When you use the record keyword to define your data class, you'll be limited by what the language allows you to do. You'll no longer have fine control over whether your data class is extensible, whether its state is mutable, the range of values that can be assigned to your fields, the accessibility to your fields, and so on. You might also be limited when it comes to having additional fields or multiple constructors.

 Data classes are still in progress at Oracle. The finer details are still being worked on. In March 2018, the datum keyword was used to define a data class but has now been changed to record.

Nowadays, developers aren't limited to working with a single programming language. Java programmers usually work with or are aware of, other programming languages that work on the JVM, such as Scala, Kotlin, or Groovy. The experience of working with varied languages brings a lot of expectations and assumptions about the capabilities and limitations of the data classes (defined using record).

Examples from the past – changes to define enums

Prior to the introduction of enums, developers often used public, static, and final variables to define constants. The following is an example:

```
class Size {
    public final static int SMALL = 1;
    public final static int MEDIUM = 2;
    public final static int LARGE = 3;
}
```

The major drawback of using `public`, `static`, `final`, and `int` variables is type safety; any `int` value could be assigned to a variable of the type `int`, instead of the `Size.SMALL`, `Size.MEDIUM`, or `Size.LARGE` constants.

Java 5 introduced enums, an addition to the language construct, to enable developers to define an enumeration of constants. Here's a quick example:

```
enum Size {SMALL, MEDIUM, LARGE}
class SmallTShirt {
    Size size = Size.SMALL;
    //..other code
}
```

With a variable of the type `Size`, an assignment is limited to the constants defined in `Size`. An enum is a perfect example of how language can simplify the implementation of a model, at the cost of certain constraints. Enums limit the extensibility to interfaces. Other than that, enums are full-fledged classes. As a developer, you can add states and behaviors to them. Another benefit is that an enum can also `switch` constructs, which was previously limited to primitives and a `String` class.

A new language construct is like a new human relationship, biological or otherwise. It has its own share of joys and sorrows.

Pattern matching with data classes

When you define your data classes using the `record` keyword, you get the added advantage of the conversion of aggregate and exploded forms of your data class. For example, the following code shows how the `switch` statement might explode the data:

```
interface Garment {}
record Button(float radius, Color color);
record Shirt(Button button, double price);
record Trousers(float length, Button button, double price);
record Cap(..)

switch (garment) {
    case Shirt(Button(var a1, var a2), Color a3): ...
    case Trousers(float a1, Button(var a2, var a3), double a4): ...
    ....
}
```

The `switch` statement can use a data class, without using its exploded form. The following code is also effective:

```
switch (garment) {
    case Shirt(Button a1, Color a2): ...
    case Trousers(float a1, Button a2, double a3): ...
    ....
}
```

Encapsulating the state

The record classes encapsulate the fields, providing default implementations of JavaBean-style accessor methods (public methods to set the values of fields). The values can be assigned during the initialization of data class instances, using their constructors.

For example, let's revisit the `Emp` data class and its decompiled version from a previous section:

```
record Emp(String name, int age) { }

final class Emp extends java.lang.DataClass {
    final String name;
    final int age;

    public Emp(String name, int age) {
        this.name = name;
        this.age = age;
    }

    // deconstructor
    // public accessor methods
    // default implementation of equals, hashCode, and toString
}
```

Abstract and non-abstract data classes

Data classes can be abstract or non-abstract. An abstract data class is defined by using the keyword `abstract` in its declaration. As an abstract class, you can't use abstract data classes directly. Here's an example of an abstract data class, `JVMLanguage`, and a non-abstract data class, `Conference`:

```
abstract record JVMLanguage(String name, int year);
record Conference(String name, String venue, DateTime when);
```

Data classes and inheritance

Currently, the proposal is to drop the following inheritance cases:

- A data class extends a regular class
- A regular class extends a data class
- A data class extends another data class

Allowing for any of the preceding cases would violate the contract of a data class being a carrier of data. At present, the following restrictions are proposed for data classes and inheritance, with interfaces and abstract data classes:

- Non-abstract and abstract data classes can extend other abstract data classes
- An abstract or non-abstract data class can extend any interface

The following figure sums up these inheritance rules:

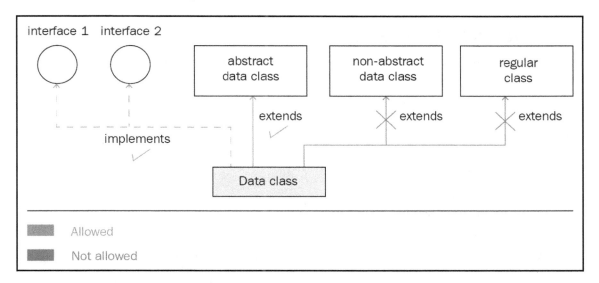

Let's get started by extending an abstract data class.

Extending an abstract data class

In the following example, the `Emp` abstract data class is being extended by the non-abstract `Manager` data class:

```
abstract record Emp(String name, int age);
record Manager(String name, int age, String country) extends Emp(name,
age);
```

When a non-abstract data class extends an abstract data class, it accepts all of the data in its header—the ones that are required for itself, and for its base class.

 A data class can extend a single abstract data class.

Implementing interfaces

A data class can implement an interface and its abstract methods, or just inherit its default methods. The following is an example:

```
interface Organizer {}
interface Speaker {
    abstract void conferenceTalk();
}

abstract record Emp(String name, int age);

record Manager(String name, int age, String country)
    extends Emp(name, age)               // subclass a record
    implements Organizer;                // implement one interface

record Programmer(String name, int age, String programmingLang)
    extends Emp(name, age)               // subclass a record
    implements Organizer, Speaker {      // implementing multiple
                                         // interfaces
        public void conferenceTalk() {   // implement abstract
                                         // method
            //.. code                    // from interface Speaker
        }
    };
```

The preceding code defines a tagging interface, `Organizer` (without any methods), and an interface, `Speaker`, with an abstract method, `conferenceTalk()`. We have two cases, as follows:

- A data class extending another data class, implementing an interface—the data class `Manager` extends the abstract `Emp` data class and implements the `Organizer` interface.
- A data class extending another data class and implementing multiple interfaces—the `Programmer` data class extends the abstract `Emp` data class and implements two interfaces—`Organizer` and `Speaker`. The `Programmer` data class must implement the abstract `conferenceTalk()` method from the `Speaker` interface to qualify as a non-abstract data class.

 A data class can implement a single or multiple interfaces.

Additional variables

Although it is allowed, before adding variables or fields to a data class, ask yourself, *Are the fields derived from the state?* Fields that are not derived from the state pose a serious violation of the initial concept of the data classes. The following code is an example that defines an additional field, `style`, derived from the state of the `Emp` data class:

```
record Emp(String name, int age) {
    private String style;
    Emp(String name, int age) {
        //.. initialize name and age
        if (age => 15 && age =< 30) style = "COOL";
        else if (age >= 31 && age <= 50) style = "SAFE";
        else if (age >= 51) style = "ELEGANT";
    }
    public String getStyle() {
        return style;
    }
}
```

The preceding code works well because the state of the `Emp` data class is still derived from its state (the `name` and `age` fields). The `getStyle` method doesn't interfere with the state of `Emp`; it is purely an implementation detail.

Overriding implicit behaviors

Suppose that you want to limit the values that can be passed to a field in your data class during its instantiation. This is feasible; just override the default constructor. The following is an example:

```
record Emp(String name, int age) {
    // override default constructor
    @Override
    public Emp(String name, int age) {
        // validate age
        if (age > 70)
            throw new IllegalArgumentException("Not employable above 70
            years");
        else {
            // call default constructor
            default.this(name, age);
        }
    }
}
```

Similarly, you can override the default implementations of object methods, such as `equals()`, `hashCode()`, and `toString()`, and other methods, such as the accessor methods.

Overriding the default behaviors of the methods of your data class doesn't defeat the purpose of their creation. They are still working as data classes, with finer control of their functionality. Let's compare this with POJOs, which were used to model data classes previously. The compiler doesn't auto-generate any methods for a POJO. So, a user still needs to read all of the code, looking for code that isn't the default implementation of its methods. In the case of data classes, this overridden behavior is very explicit. So, a user doesn't have to worry about reading all of the code; they can assume default implementation of the behavior, which hasn't been overridden by the developer.

 Overriding behavior explicitly states the places where a data class diverts from its default behavior, reducing the amount of code that must be read by a user to understand its behavior.

Additional methods and constructors

The compiler generates a default constructor for a data class, along with accessor methods and the default implementation of the methods from the object class. A developer can overload the constructors and add more methods to a data class, as follows:

```
record Emp(String name, int age) {
    // overloading constructor
    public Emp(String name, String style) {
            this.name = name;
            if (style.equals("COOL") age = 20;
            else if (style.equals("SAFE") age = 30;
            else if (style.equals("ELEGANT") age = 50;
            else age = 70;
        }
    }
    public String fancyOutput() {                    // additional method
        return "My style is COOL";
    }
}
```

Mutability

Concerning whether the data classes should be designated as mutable or immutable, work is still in progress. Both options have advantages and disadvantages. Immutable data works well in multithreaded, parallel, or concurrent systems. On the other hand, mutable data works well with cases that require frequent modifications to data.

 Concerning thread safety, since the data classes are not yet designated to be immutable, it is the responsibility of the developers to use them in thread-safe configurations.

Summary

In this chapter, we covered the challenges of using POJOs to model data. We covered how data classes provide a simple and concise way to model data. This will include language changes, with the introduction of the `record` keyword. The main goal of using data classes is to model data as data, not to reduce the boilerplate code.

We also covered the aggregate and exploded forms of data classes. The data classes can be used with other language constructs, such as `switch`. By default, the data classes are not mutable, including the arrays defined as the data members. Since these structures are not immutable, a developer must include code to ensure thread safety when working with them.

In the next chapter, you'll learn more about an exciting language enhancement—raw string literals. Does this mean a pure, or untouched, string? Find out for yourself by reading on.

15
Raw String Literals

Have you ever felt the pain of using string types to store SQL queries in Java, with multiple opening and closing, single and double quotes? To add to the misery, perhaps you have used newline escape sequences and concatenation operators. Similar discomfort applies to using string types with HTML, XML, or JSON code. If you dread all of these combinations like I do, fear no more. Raw string literals are here to save you from the pain.

With raw string literals, you can easily work with readable, multiline string values, without including special newline indicators. Since raw string literals don't interpret escape sequences, it is simple to include escape sequences as part of the string values. The related classes also include management of margins.

In this chapter, we'll cover the following topics:

- The advantages and difficulties of using escape sequences in string values
- New methods added to the `String` class
- Margin management
- Delimiters
- Examples of using raw strings with varied multiline text data

Technical requirements

The code in this chapter will use raw string literals, which are meant for JDK 12 (Mar 2019). You can clone the repository that includes raw string literals to experiment with it.

All of the code in this chapter can be accessed at `https://github.com/PacktPublishing/Java-11-and-12-New-Features`.

A quick example

Are you excited to see raw strings in action? I am. Let's look at a quick example, before diving into the problems that led to the introduction of raw strings.

The following code shows how you can write a multiline string value with raw string literals, using a backtick (`` ` ``) as the delimiter, without using a concatenation operator or special indicators for a newline or tab:

```
String html =
`<HTML>
    <BODY>
        <H1>Meaning of life</H1>
    </BODY>
</HTML>
`;
```

Issues with existing multiline string values

The creation of multiline string values is common in most programming languages, including Java. You might use them to create HTML code, a JSON or XML value, or an SQL query. But this seemingly simple task becomes complicated with the use of escape sequences (of newline or tab indicators).

To make your multiline string values readable, you might define parts of your string values on separate lines, using the concatenation operator (+) to glue them together. However, with increasing string lengths, this can become difficult to write and comprehend.

Let's outline the simple task of creating a multiline string, and then use multiple approaches to store it as a string value.

A simple task

Suppose that you have to define the following multiline value using the string type, keeping its indentation in place:

```
<HTML>
    <BODY>
            <H1>Meaning of life</H1>
    </BODY>
</HTML>
```

Escape sequence hell with traditional string literals

To add a newline or tab to a traditional string value, you can use the escape sequences \n and \t. Escape sequences are letters preceded with \ (a backslash), and they have a special meaning in Java. For example in Java strings, \n is used as a newline, and \t is used as a tab.

 An escape sequence is a letter combination used for values that can't be represented directly. For instance, to use the newline control character from ASCII, Java uses \n. Java defines multiple other escape sequences.

The following code shows how you can store the multiline string value with newline and tab escape sequences. The newline and tab escape sequences will include the indentation in the variable HTML:

```
String html = "<HTML>\n\t<BODY>\n\t\t<H1>Meaning in
life</H1>\n\t</BODY>\n</HTML>";
```

As you can see, the preceding can be difficult to write. You'll have to figure out the newlines and count the tabs in the target string value, and insert them as \n or \t. Another challenge is reading this code. You'll have to try to figure out line by line what the code is intended to do.

Concatenation hell with traditional string literals

The following is an alternative that is meant to make the preceding code readable, by defining parts of the string value on multiple lines. However, when doing so, you should use multiple string concatenation operators (+) and string delimiters ("):

```
String html =   "<HTML>" +
"\n\t" + "<BODY>" +
"\n\t\t" + "<H1>Meaning of life</H1>" +
"\n\t" + "</BODY>" +
"\n" + "</HTML>";
```

I would prefer to add whitespaces to the preceding code, to make it more readable:

```
String html =   "<HTML>" +
                    "\n\t" + "<BODY>" +
                        "\n\t\t" + "<H1>Meaning of life</H1>" +
                    "\n\t" + "</BODY>" +
               "\n" + "</HTML>";
```

Although the preceding code looks better in terms of readability, it delegates a lot of responsibility to the programmer, to insert whitespaces in the correct places. As a quick note, the whitespaces (outside of the double quotes) aren't a part of the variable HTML; they just make it readable. As a developer, it's a pain to write such code.

 The Java GUI library doesn't work with the control characters, such as the newline. So, this approach can be used with GUI classes.

Including escape sequences as part of string values

Imagine what happens when the letter combination represented by an escape sequence (let's say, \n) must be included as a part of the string value. Let's modify our example, as follows:

```
<HTML>
    <BODY>
            <H1>\n - new line, \t - tab</H1>
    </BODY>
</HTML>
```

In this case, you can escape the \n sequence by using another backslash, as follows:

```
String html =   "<HTML>" +
                    "\n\t" + "<BODY>" +
                        "\n\t\t" + "<H1>\\n - new line, \\t - tab</H1>"
                        +
                    "\n\t" + "</BODY>" +
               "\n" + "</HTML>";
```

But, with the changes, it's getting difficult to read and understand the preceding code. Imagine a developer in your team writes such code. Let's see how you could make it more readable.

As a workaround, you can define `String` constants (say, `tab` or `newLine`), assigning the values of \t and \n to them. You can use these constants instead of the literal values of \n and \t in the preceding code. This replacement will make the code easier to read.

Strings and regex patterns, another hell

This section will provide another example of escaping sequence hell—defining regex patterns as Java strings.

To remove whitespaces (spaces or tabs) between a word character and a period (`.`), you'll need the following **regex (regular expression)** pattern:

```
(\w)(\s+))[\.]
```

To store it using a Java string, you'll need the following code:

```
String patternToMatch = "(\\w)(\\s+)([\\.,])";     // Isn't that a lot
                                                   // to digest?
                                                   // Does the regex
                                                   // pattern has
                                                   // a single
                                                   // backslash, or,
                                                   // two of them?
```

I'll share a quick secret here—when I started working with Java, one of my biggest nightmares was defining patterns as string values. I admit it; I had a difficulty writing patterns, and using the \ escape character with the sequences in my patterns made my life miserable.

 This is also referred to as **leaning toothpick syndrome** (**LTS**)—making string values unreadable by using a lot of backslashes.

Let's put an end to this string misery by using raw string literals.

Welcoming raw string literals

The raw string literals are non-interpreted string literals. In real-world projects, you would need to work with literal string values as is, without any special handling of the Unicode values, backslashes, or newlines. Raw string literals set aside Java escapes and Java line terminator specifications, in order to make the code readable and maintainable.

Rewriting using raw strings

You can define a multiline string value by using raw literals, as follows:

```
String html =
`<HTML>
    <BODY>
        <H1>Meaning of life</H1>
    </BODY>
</HTML>
`;
```

By using ` as the opening and closing delimiter, you can define multiline string literals with ease and elegance.

The preceding code is free from Java indicators (concatenation operators or escape sequences).

The delimiter (backtick)

A raw string literal is defined as follows:

```
RawStringDelimeter {RawStringCharacters} RawStringDelimeter
```

A backtick is used as the delimiter for raw string literals. I believe that using ` for raw string literals is a good decision. The ` backtick looks like ' (a single quote) and " (a double quote), which have been used as delimiters for character and string literals. The ` backtick will help Java programmers to easily see it as a delimiter for raw strings.

 A raw string literal uses ` as a delimiter. A traditional string literal uses " as a delimiter and a character uses ' as a delimiter.

If you wish to include one backtick as a part of the string value, you can use two backticks
(` `` `) to define your value. This works for *n* number of backticks; just make sure to match the
count of opening and closing backticks. This sounds interesting. Let's look at an example
that includes ` ` ` as part of its value:

```
String html =
``<HTML>
    <BODY>
        <H1>I think I like ` as a delimiter!</H1>
    </BODY>
</HTML>
``;
```

The following is another example, which uses multiple backticks in the string value and as
delimiters. Of course, the count of backticks included in the string value is not equal to the
count of backticks used as delimiters:

```
String html =
````<HTML>
    <BODY>
        <H1>I believe I would have liked ``` too(!)</H1>
    </BODY>
</HTML>
````;
```

If there is a mismatch between the count of backticks in the opening and
closing delimiters, the code won't compile.

# Treating escape values

The Unicode and escape sequences are never interpreted in a raw string literal value.

A lexer is a software program that performs **lexical analysis**. Lexical analysis is the process
of tokenizing a stream of characters into words and tokens. As you read this line, you are
analyzing this string lexically, using the spaces to separate chunks of letters as words.

This analysis is disabled for the raw string literals at the start of the opening backtick. It is
re-enabled at the closing backtick.

Don't replace the backtick in your string value with its Unicode escape (that is, `\u0060 in`), for consistency.

The only exceptions to this rule are CR (carriage return—`\u000D`) and CRLF (carriage return and line feed—`\u000D\u000A`). Both of these are translated to LF (line feed—`\u000A`).

# Raw string literals versus traditional string literals

The introduction of raw string literals will not change the interpretation of the traditional string literal values. This includes their multiline capabilities and how they handle the escape sequences and delimiters. A traditional string can include Unicode escapes (JLS 3.3) or escape sequences (JLS 3.10.6).

A Java class file, that is, the Java bytecode, does not record whether a string constant was created using a traditional string or a raw string. Both traditional and raw string values are stored as instances of the `java.lang.String` class.

# Interpreting escape sequences

To interpret escape sequences in multiline raw string values, Java will add methods to the String class—`unescape()` and `escape()`:

```
public String unescape() {...}
public String escape() {...}
```

 Considering raw string literals at Oracle, work is in progress. Oracle is considering swapping the names of the methods `unescape()` and `escape()`, or even renaming them.

# The unescape() method

By default, the raw string literals don't interpret the escape sequences. However, what if you want them to do so? When used with a raw string, the `unescape()` method will match the sequence of the characters following \ with the sequence of Unicode escapes and escape sequences, as defined in the **Java Language Specifications** (**JLS**). If a match is found, the escape sequence will not be used as a regular combination of letters; it will be used as an escape sequence.

The following code doesn't interpret \n as a newline escape sequence:

```
System.out.print("eJava");
System.out.print("\\n");
System.out.print("Guru");
```

The output of the preceding code is as follows:

**eJava\nGuru**

However, the following code will interpret \n as a newline escape sequence:

```
System.out.print("eJava");
System.out.print(`\n`.unescape());       // Don't ignore the escape char
System.out.print("Guru");
```

The output of the preceding code will provide the eJava and Guru string values on separate lines, as follows:

**eJava**
**Guru**

When interpreted as escape sequences, a combination of letters that is used to represent them, is counted as a control character of the length 1. The output of the following code will be 1:

```
System.out.print(`\n`.unescape().length());
```

## The escape() method

The `escape()` method will be used to invert the escapes. The following table shows how it will convert the characters:

| Original character | Converted character |
|---|---|
| Less than ' ' (space) | Unicode or character escape sequences |
| Above ~ (tilde) | Unicode escape sequences |
| " (double quotes) | Escape sequence |
| ' (single quote) | Escape sequence |
| \ (backslash) | Escape sequence |

The following example doesn't include a newline in the output:

```
System.out.println("eJava" + "\n".escape() + "Guru");
```

The output of the preceding code is as follows:

```
eJava\nGuru
```

Consider the following code:

```
System.out.println("eJava" + `•`.escape());
```

The output of the preceding code is as follows (• is converted to its equivalent escape value):

```
eJava\u2022Guru
```

# Managing margins

Suppose that you have to import multiline text from a file in your Java code. How would you prefer to treat the margins of the imported text? You may have to align or indent the imported text. The text might use a custom newline delimiter (say, [), which you might prefer to strip from the text. To work with these requirements, a set of new methods, such as `align()`, `indent()`, and `transform()`, are being added to the `String` class, which we'll cover in the next section.

# The align() method

When you define a multiline string value, you might choose to format the string against the left margin or align it with the indentation used by the code. The string values are stored with the margin intact. The `align()` method will provide incidental indentation support; it will strip off any leading or trailing blank lines, then justify each line, without losing the indentations.

The following is an example:

```
String comment =
        `one
           of
                      my
             favorite
                 lang
                      feature
        from Amber(!)
`.align();
System.out.println(comment);
```

The output of the preceding code is as follows:

```
one
   of
              my
    favorite
        lang
            feature
from Amber(!)
```

# The indent(int) method

The `indent(int)` method will enable developers to specify custom indentations for their multiline string values. You can pass a positive number, i, to `indent(int)`, to add i spaces (U+0020) to your text, or you can pass a negative number, to remove a given number of whitespaces from each line of your multiline text.

An example is as follows:

```
String comment =
        `one
           of
                      my
             favorite
```

```
        lang
             feature
     from Amber(!)
`.align().indent(15);
System.out.println(comment);
```

The output of the preceding code is as follows:

```
one
    of
            my
        favorite
            lang
                feature
    from Amber(!)
```

 The indent(int) method can be used to add or remove whitespaces from each line in a multitext value. By passing a positive number, you can add whitespaces, and you can remove them by passing negative values.

## The overloaded align(int) method

The align(int) method will first align the rows of a multistring value, and will then indent it with the specified spaces. The following is an example:

```
String comment =
        `one
          of
                    my
            favorite
                lang
                    feature
        from Amber(!)
`.align(15);
System.out.println(comment);
```

The output of the preceding code is as follows (the text on each line is preceded by fifteen spaces):

```
one
    of
            my
        favorite
            lang
                feature
```

```
from Amber(!)
```

# The detab(int) and entab methods

A tab (U+0009) usually represents four whitespaces (U+0020). However, not all of the applications convert between tabs and whitespaces when they use text that includes a mix of whitespaces and tabs. To combat this challenge with the multiline text, the String class will include two methods, detab(int) and entab(int), which will convert a tab to whitespaces, and vice versa:

```
public String detab(int)
public String entab(int)
```

Let's modify the preceding example, so that the content includes tabs instead of whitespaces, as follows:

```
String comment =
        `one
    of
            my
        favorite
            lang
    feature
    from Amber(!)
`.detab(1);
```

The output of the preceding code is as follows (each tab is converted to one whitespace):

```
  one
of
  my
 favorite
  lang
feature
from Amber(!)
```

# The transform() method

Suppose that a file includes the following text, using [ at the beginning of a new line:

```
[ Talks - Java11, Amber, CleanCode
[ Oceans - plastic pollution, human callousness
```

Now, suppose that you must remove the delimiter, [, used at the beginning of all lines. You can use the `transform()` method to customize the margin management, adding the `String` class:

```
<R> R transform (Function<String, R> f)
```

The following is an example that uses the method `transform()` to remove the custom margin characters from the multiline text:

```
String stripped = `
                  [ Talks - Java11, Amber, CleanCode
                  [ Oceans - dying, human callousness, plastic
                  pollution
            `.transform({
              multiLineText.stream()
                  .map(e -> e.map(String::strip)
                  .map(s -> s.startsWith("[  ") ?
                      s.substring("[  ".length())
                      : s)
                  .collect(Collectors.joining("\n", "", "\n"));
            });
```

The next section will include some common cases where using raw string literals over traditional strings will benefit you tremendously.

# Common examples

If you have used stored JSON, XML data, database queries, or file paths as string literals, you know it is difficult to write and read such code. This section will highlight examples of how a traditional raw string will improve the readability of your code when working with these types of data.

## JSON data

Suppose that you have the following JSON data to be stored as a Java string:

```
{"plastic": {
  "id": "98751",
  "singleuse": {
    "item": [
      {"value": "Water Bottle", "replaceWith": "Steel Bottle()"},
      {"value": "Straw", "replaceWith": "Ban Straws"},
      {"value": "Spoon", "replaceWith": "Steel Spoon"}
```

```
        ]
    }
} }
```

The following code shows how you would perform this action with the traditional `String` class, escaping the double quotes within the data by using \ and adding a newline escape sequence:

```
String data =
"{\"plastic\": { \n" +
  "\"id\": \"98751\", \n" +
  "\"singleuse\": { \n" +
    "\"item\": [ \n" +
      "{\"value\": \"Water Bottle\", \"replaceWith\": \"Steel
        Bottle()\"}, \n" +
      "{\"value\": \"Straw\", \"replaceWith\": \"Ban Straws\"}, \n" +
      "{\"value\": \"Spoon\", \"replaceWith\": \"Steel Spoon\"} \n" +
    "] \n" +
  "} \n" +
"}}";
```

To be honest, it took me quite a while to write the preceding code, escaping the double quotes with the backslash. As you can see, this code is not readable.

The following example shows how you can code the same JSON data using raw string literals, without giving up the code readability:

```
String data =
```{"plastic": {
  "id": "98751",
  "singleuse": {
    "item": [
      {"value": "Water Bottle", "replaceWith": "Steel Bottle()"},
      {"value": "Straw", "replaceWith": "Ban Straws"},
      {"value": "Spoon", "replaceWith": "Steel Spoon"}
    ]
  }
}}```;
```
```

# XML data

The following code is an example of XML data that you might need to store using a Java string:

```
<plastic id="98751">
  <singleuse>
    <item value="Water Bottle" replaceWith="Steel bottle" />
    <item value="Straw" replaceWith="Ban Straws" />
    <item value="spoon" replaceWith="Steel Spoon" />
  </singleuse>
</plastic>
```

The following code shows how you can define the preceding data as a String literal by using the appropriate escape sequences:

```
String data =
"<plastic id=\"98751\">\n" +
  "<singleuse>\n" +
    "<item value=\"Water Bottle\" replaceWith=\"Steel bottle\" />\n" +
    "<item value=\"Straw\" replaceWith=\"Ban Straws\" />\n" +
    "<item value=\"spoon\" replaceWith=\"Steel Spoon\" />\n" +
  "</singleuse>\n" +
"</plastic>";
```

Again, the escape sequences added to the preceding code (\ to escape " and \n to add newline) make it very difficult to read and understand the code. The following example shows how you can drop the programming-specific details from the data by using raw string literals:

```
String dataUsingRawStrings =
```
<plastic id="98751">
  <singleuse>
    <item value="Water Bottle" replaceWith="Steel bottle" />
    <item value="Straw" replaceWith="Ban Straws" />
    <item value="spoon" replaceWith="Steel Spoon" />
  </singleuse>
</plastic>
```;
```

# File paths

The file paths on Windows OS use a backslash to separate the directories and their subdirectories. For instance, `C:\Mala\eJavaGuru` refers to the `eJavaGuru` subdirectory in the `Mala` directory in the `C:` drive. Here's how you can store this path by using a traditional string literal:

```
String filePath = "C:\\Mala\\eJavaGuru\\ocp11.txt";
```

With raw string literals, you can store the same file path as follows (changes are highlighted in bold):

```
String rawFilePath = `C:\Mala\eJavaGuru\ocp11.txt`;
```

# Database queries

Suppose that you have to create an SQL query that includes the column names, table names, and literal values. The following code shows how you would typically write it, using traditional strings:

```
String query = "SELECT talk_title, speaker_name " +
               "FROM    talks, speakers " +
               "WHERE   talks.speaker_id = speakers.speaker_id " +
               "AND     talks.duration > 50 ";
```

You can also write the code as follows, using quotes around the column or table names, depending on the target database management system:

```
String query = "SELECT 'talk_title', 'speaker_name' " +
               "FROM    'talks', 'speakers' " +
               "WHERE   'talks.speaker_id' = 'speakers.speaker_id' " +
               "AND     'talks.duration' > 50 ";
```

The raw string literal values are much more readable, as shown in the following code:

```
String query =
```SELECT 'talk_title', 'speaker_name'
   FROM    'talks', 'speakers'
   WHERE   'talks.speaker_id' = 'speakers.speaker_id'
   AND     'talks.duration' > 50
```;
```

# Summary

In this chapter, we covered the challenges that developers face when storing various types of multiline text values as string values. Raw string literals address these concerns. They also significantly improve the writability and readability of multiline string values by disabling the lexical analysis of escape characters and escape sequences. Raw string literals will introduce multiple methods to the `String` class, such as `unescape()`, `escape()`, `align()`, `indent()`, and `transform()`. Together, these methods enable developers to specifically process the raw string literals.

In the next chapter, we'll cover how the lambda leftovers project is improving the functional programming syntax and experience in Java.

# 16
# Lambda Leftovers

Imagine the convenience of marking unused parameters in a method or lambda expression and not passing any arbitrary values to conform to the syntax. Also, when working with lambdas, imagine the ability to declare a lambda parameter name, without caring whether the same variable name has been used in the enclosing scope or not. This is what **lambda leftovers** (JEP 302) provide in order to enhance lambdas and method references. Apart from these enhancements, it will also offer better disambiguation of functional expressions in methods (this is marked as optional in the **JDK Enhancement Proposal** (**JEP**), as of right now).

In this chapter, we'll cover the following topics:

- Using underscores for unused method parameters
- Shadowing lambda parameters
- Disambiguation of functional expressions

## Technical requirements

The code in this chapter will use the features defined in lambda leftovers (JEP 302), which has yet to be targeted for a JDK release version. To experiment with the code, you can clone the relevant repository.

All of the code in this chapter can be accessed at `https://github.com/PacktPublishing/Java-11-and-12-New-Features`.

Let's get started by understanding why would you need to mark unused lambda parameters.

# Marking unused parameters with underscores

Suppose that you are served four food items at a restaurant, but you don't eat three of them. If the restaurant has a protocol for customers to mark **ort** (which literally means *used*) and non-ort food items, the food from the table can be used in a certain manner. For example, the restaurant can mark the non-ort items as *good to eat*, and can consider sharing them with the needy.

Similarly, when calling a method or a lambda expression, you might not need all of the method parameters. In that case, communicating your intent to the compiler (that certain parameters aren't used) is a good idea. This has two benefits—it saves the compiler from type-checking the values that are not required, and it saves you from passing any arbitrary values to match the code definition and code-calling syntax.

## An example of lambda parameters

The following is an example to demonstrate how you can use an _ (underscore) to mark unused lambda parameters. The following code uses the BiFunction<T, U, R> functional interface which can accept two arguments (T and U), and returns a value of the type R:

```
BiFunction<Integer, String, Boolean> calc = (age, _) -> age > 10;
```

In the preceding example, since the lambda expression assigned to the BiFunction functional interface uses just one of the method parameters (that is, age), JEP 302 proposes using the underscore to mark the unused parameter.

The following code highlights a few use cases to illustrate how you would use the same code without the convenience of marking unused lambda parameters (the comments state the value that the code is passing to the unused parameter):

```
// Approach 1
// Pass null to the unused parameter
BiFunction<Boolean, Integer, String> calc = (age, null) -> age > 10;

// Approach 2
// Pass empty string to the unused parameter
BiFunction<Boolean, Integer, String> calc = (age, "") -> age > 10;

// Approach 3
// Pass ANY String value to the unused parameter -
```

```
// - doesn't matter, since it is not used
BiFunction<Boolean, Integer, String> calc =
                       (age, "Ban plastic straws") -> age > 10;

// Approach 4
// Pass any variable (of the same type) to the unused parameter -
// - doesn't matter, since it is not used
BiFunction<Boolean, Integer, String> calc = (age, name) -> age > 10;
```

A lot of other functional programming languages use a similar notation to mark unused parameters.

# The journey of getting there

Using an underscore to mark unused parameters required changes in the Java language.

Until Java 8, the underscore was used as a valid identifier. The first step was to deny permission to use an underscore as a regular identifier. So, Java 8 issued a compiler warning for the usage of _ as the name of formal parameters in lambdas. This was simple, and had no backward-compatibility issues since lambdas were introduced in Java 8. Moving forward, Java 9 replaced the compiler warning message with compilation errors for using underscores as parameter names.

With JEP 302, developers can use _ to mark an unused method parameter for the following:

- Lambdas
- Methods
- Catch handlers

In the next section, you'll see how (in the future) your lambda parameters will be able to shadow the variables with the same name in their enclosing scopes.

# Shadowing of lambda parameters

Java doesn't allow the declaration of variables with the same names in multiple scenarios. For instance, you can't define instance and static variables in a class with the same name. Similarly, you can't define method parameters and local variables with the same names in a method.

However, you can define local variables with the same names as an instance or `static` variables in a class. This doesn't mean that you can't access them later. To access an instance variable from a method, you can prefix the variable name with the `this` keyword.

These restrictions allow you to access all of the variables within a scope.

# The existing case of lambda parameters

When you write a lambda expression, you can define multiple parameters. The following are some examples of lambdas that define single or multiple parameters:

```
key -> key.uppercase();            // single lambda parameter
(int x, int y) -> x > y? x : y;    // two lambda parameters
(a, b, c, d) -> a + b + c + d;     // four lambda parameters
```

Let's use one of the lambdas from the preceding code in stream processing. The following example will provide the string values from `List` as output, in uppercase:

```
List<String> talks = List.of("Kubernetes", "Docker", "Java 11");
talks.stream()
        .map(key -> key.toUpperCase())
        .forEach(System.out::prinltn);
```

So far, so good. But what happens if the preceding code is defined in a method (say, `process()`) with a local variable (say, `key` (code on line number 3)) that overlaps with the name of the `key` lambda parameter (defined and used on the line number 5)? See the following code:

```
1. void process() {
2.     List<String> talks = List.of("Kubernetes", "Docker", "Java 11");
3.     String key = "Docker"; // local variable key
4.     talks.stream()
5.         .map(key -> key.toUpperCase())         // WON'T compile: 'key'
               redefined
6.         .forEach(System.out::prinltn);
7. }
```

At present, the preceding code won't compile, because the `key` variable used in the lambda expression for the `map()` method can't overshadow the local `key` variable, defined in the `process()` method.

# Why should lambda parameters overshadow enclosing variables?

When you write a lambda expression, you (usually) define the parameter names as indicators of how the values assigned to them should be processed. They aren't meant to reuse the existing values, referred to by variables, in an enclosing block.

Let's revisit the preceding code:

```
1. String key = "Docker"; // local variable key
2. talks.stream()
3.     .map(key -> key.toUpperCase())        // WON'T compile : 'key'
                                              // redefined
4.     .forEach(System.out::println);
```

In the preceding code, the lambda expression on line 3 (in bold) defines one lambda parameter, key, specifying that when a value is passed to it, Java should call the toUpperCase() method on it and return the resulting value.

As is evident from this example, the key lambda parameter appears to be unrelated to the local key variable, defined in the enclosing block. So, the lambda parameters should be allowed to overshadow the variables with the same names in the enclosing block.

# A few of the known issues

As of now, it isn't clear whether a lambda expression will be able to access the value of the enclosing variable, which is overshadowed by the lambda parameter; and if it can, how?

For example, let's modify the preceding code by replacing the call to the toUppercase() method with a call to the concat() method as follows (changes are in bold):

```
1. String key = "Docker"; // local variable key
2. talks.stream()
3.     .map(key -> key.concat(key))
4.     .forEach(System.out::prinltn);
```

In the preceding code, imagine that the lambda expression on line 3 needs to access the value of the key variable defined on line 1, since it wants to pass it to the concat() method. As of right now, it hasn't been finalized whether this will be allowed.

If it is allowed, Java will need to devise a way to mark and clearly differentiate a lambda parameter from another variable with the same name, in the enclosing block. This will be required for code readability—which, as you know, is important.

 The accessibility of the overshadowed enclosing variable is the main problem associated with shadowing of lambda parameters.

In the next section, we'll look at how Java is trying to resolve overloaded method calls, which define functional interfaces as parameters.

# Disambiguation of functional expressions

If you think Java started its journey through type inference with the var keyword (Java 10), think again. Type inference was introduced with Java 5 and has been increasing in coverage ever since.

With Java 8, the resolution of overloaded methods was restructured to allow for working with type inference. Before the introduction of lambdas and method references, a call to a method was resolved by checking the types of the arguments that were passed to it (the return type wasn't considered).

With Java 8, implicit lambdas and implicit method references couldn't be checked for the types of values that they accepted, leading to restricted compiler capabilities, to rule out ambiguous calls to overloaded methods. However, explicit lambdas and method references could still be checked by their arguments by the compiler. For your information, the lambdas that explicitly specify the types of their parameters are termed **explicit lambdas**.

Limiting the compiler's ability and relaxing the rules in this way was purposeful. It lowered the cost of type-checking for lambdas and avoided brittleness.

 Although it is an interesting feature, the disambiguation of functional expressions is slated as an optional feature in JEP 302, because Oracle needs to assess its impact on the compiler implementation.

Before diving into the proposed solution, let's look at the existing issues, using code examples.

# Issues with resolving overloaded methods – passing lambdas

Let's cover the existing issues with resolving overloaded methods when lambdas are passed as method parameters. Let's define two interfaces, `Swimmer` and `Diver`, as follows:

```
interface Swimmer {
    boolean test(String lap);
}
interface Diver {
    String dive(int height);
}
```

In the following code, the overloaded `evaluate` method accepts the interfaces `Swimmer` and `Diver` as method parameters:

```
class SwimmingMeet {
    static void evaluate(Swimmer swimmer) {    // code compiles
        System.out.println("evaluate swimmer");
    }
    static void evaluate(Diver diver) {      // code compiles
        System.out.println("evaluate diver");
    }
}
```

Let's call the overloaded `evaluate()` method in the following code:

```
class FunctionalDisambiguation {
    public static void main(String args[]) {
        SwimmingMeet.evaluate(a -> false); // This code WON'T compile
    }
}
```

Revisit the lambda from the preceding code:

```
    a -> false                             // this is an implicit lambda
```

Since the preceding lambda expression doesn't specify the type of its input parameter, it could be either `String` (the `test()` method and the `Swimmer` interface) or `int` (the `dive()` method and the `Diver` interface). Since the call to the `evaluate()` method is ambiguous, it doesn't compile.

Let's add the type of the method parameter to the preceding code, making it an explicit lambda:

```
SwimmingMeet.evaluate((String a) -> false);        // This compiles!!
```

The preceding call is not ambiguous now; the lambda expression accepts an input parameter of the String type and returns a boolean value, which maps to the evaluate() method which accepts Swimmer as a parameter (the functional test() method in the Swimmer interface accepts a parameter of the String type).

Let's see what happens if the Swimmer interface is modified, changing the data type of the lap parameter from String to int. To avoid confusion, all of the code will be repeated, with the modifications in bold:

```
interface Swimmer {                                 // test METHOD IS
                                                    // MODIFIED
    boolean test(int lap);     // String lap changed to int lap
}
interface Diver {
    String dive(int height);
}
class SwimmingMeet {
    static void evaluate(Swimmer swimmer) {        // code compiles
        System.out.println("evaluate swimmer");
    }
    static void evaluate(Diver diver) {            // code compiles
        System.out.println("evaluate diver");
    }
}
```

Consider the following code, thinking about which of the lines of code will compile:

```
1. SwimmingMeet.evaluate(a -> false);
2. SwimmingMeet.evaluate((int a) -> false);
```

In the preceding example, the code on both of the line numbers won't compile for the same reason—the compiler is unable to determine the call to the overloaded evaluate() method. Since both of the functional methods (that is, test() in the Swimmer interface and dive() in the Diver interface) accept one method parameter of the int type, it isn't feasible for the compiler to determine the method call.

As a developer, you might argue that since the return types of `test()` and `dive()` are different, the compiler should be able to infer the correct calls. Just to reiterate, the return types of a method don't participate in method overloading. Overloaded methods must return in the count or type of their parameters.

> The return type of methods doesn't participate in method overloading. Overloaded methods must return in the count or type of their parameters.

# Issues with resolving overloaded methods – passing method references

You can define overloaded methods with different parameter types, as follows:

```
class Championship {
    static boolean reward(Integer lapTime) {
        return(lapTime < 60);
    }
    static boolean reward(String lap) {
        return(lap.equalsIgnoreCase("final ");
    }
}
```

However, the following code doesn't compile:

```
someMethod(Chamionship::reward);                    // ambiguous call
```

In the preceding line of code, since the compiler is not allowed to examine the method reference, the code fails to compile. This is unfortunate since the method parameters to the overloaded methods are `Integer` and `String`—no value can be compatible with both.

# The proposed solution

The accidental compiler issues involved with overloaded methods that use either lambda expressions or method references can be resolved by allowing the compiler to consider their return type as `also`. The compiler would then be able to choose the right overloaded method and eliminate the unmatched option.

# Summary

For Java developers working with lambdas and method references, this chapter demonstrates what Java has in the pipeline to help ease problems.

Lambda Leftovers (JEP 302) proposes using an underscore for unused parameters in lambdas, methods, and catch handlers. It plans to allow developers to define lambda parameters that can overshadow variables with the same name in their enclosing block. The disambiguation of functional expressions is an important and powerful feature. It will allow compilers to consider the return types of lambdas in order to determine the right overloaded methods. Since it can affect how the compilers work, this feature is marked as optional in this JEP.

In the next chapter, which is on pattern matching and switch expressions, you'll get to know the exciting capabilities that are being added to the Java language.

 This chapter didn't include any coding exercises for the reader. The return type of methods doesn't participate in method overloading. Overloaded methods must return in the count or type of their parameters.

# 17
# Pattern Matching

As a Java programmer, imagine having the option of skipping usage of the `instanceof` operator and explicit casting operators to retrieve a value from your objects. Pattern matching (**JDK Enhancement Proposals (JEP)** 305) addresses this pain point by adding type test patterns and constant patterns. It enhances the Java programming language to introduce functionality that enables you to determine the type of instances and derived classes, and access their members without using explicit casting.

In this chapter, we'll cover the following topics:

- Pattern matching
- Type test patterns
- Constant patterns

## Technical requirements

The code in this chapter uses the features defined in pattern matching (JEP 305) that haven't been targeted for any JDK release version yet. To experiment with the code, you can clone the relevant repository.

All code in this chapter can be accessed at `https://github.com/PacktPublishing/Java-11-and-12-New-Features`.

Let's cover the issues with using `instanceof` and explicit type-casting operators.

# Pattern matching

Pattern matching will enhance the Java programming language. To start with, it will add type test patterns and constant patterns that will be supported by the `switch` statement and the `matches` expression. Later, this JEP might extend the supported patterns and language construct.

Pattern matching is an age-old technique (approximately 65 years old) that has been adapted and is used by various languages such as text-oriented, functional (Haskell), and object-oriented languages (Scala, C#).

A pattern is a combination of the following:

- A predicate
- A target
- A set of binding variables

When a predicate is successfully applied to a target, a set of binding variables are extracted from the target. The patterns covered in this chapter are type test patterns and constant patterns.

Before working with the examples in detail, let's understand what the existing issues are and why we need pattern matching.

# Existing issues with type testing

As a Java developer, you should have worked with code such as the one highlighted in bold in the following block:

```
Object obj = new Ocean();                               // variable type - Object
if (obj instanceof Ocean) {                             // check instance type
    System.out.println(((Ocean)obj).getBottles());      // cast & extract value
}
// A basic class - Ocean
class Ocean {
   private long bottles;
   public long getBottles() {
        return bottles;
   }
}
```

The preceding code includes three steps to use the value of the `bottles` variable:

1. `obj instanceof Ocean`: Testing of the type of the `obj` variable
2. `(Ocean)obj`: Casting of the reference variable, `obj`, to `Ocean`
3. `((Ocean)obj).getBottles()`: Destruction of the instance to get a value

As developers, we have been writing similar code for a long time, but have also been hating it secretly. It is like repeating the same instructions again and again. These steps to test, cast, and deconstruct an instance to extract a value are unnecessarily verbose. We all know that code repetition is one of the best ways for errors to go unnoticed. To add to this, it only gets bigger with multiple instances of code repetition in one place. Take the following code sample as an example:

```
void dyingFish(Object obj) {
    if (obj instanceof Ocean) {                          // test
        System.out.println(((Ocean)obj).getBottles());   // cast &
                                                          // destruct
    }
    else if (obj instanceof Sea) {                       // test
        System.out.println(((Sea)obj).getDeadFish());
    }
    else if (obj instanceof River) {                     // test
        if ( ((Ocean)obj).getPlasticBags() > 100) {      // cast &
                                                          // destruct
            System.out.println("Say no to plastic bags. Fish are dying!");
        }
    }
}
class Ocean { .. }
class Sea { .. }
class River { .. }
```

As you add more occurrences of the testing-casting-instance destruction pattern to retrieve the field values, you lose the business logic in the complexity that is induced by the language. It is very common for developers to literally copy and paste such code and modify the pieces that aren't the same—but it is also common for some code parts to be left unchanged (which either become logic errors or should be labeled as copy and paste errors).

This code is also less optimizable; it will have $O(n)$ time complexity, even though the underlying problem is often $O(1)$.

# Type test patterns

To get around the issues created by the testing-casting-instance destruction pattern, Java proposes to embrace pattern matching.

Here's an example of the proposed changes to the language:

```
Object obj = new Ocean();                       // variable type - Object
if (obj matches Ocean o) {                       // check & bind
    System.out.println(o.getBottles());          // extract
}
```

The preceding code introduces a new Java keyword, matches, which includes a **predicate** (obj) and a **target** (Ocean o). The predicate, that is, obj is applied to the target, that is, Ocean o, which binds the o variable to the instance referred by obj. If the matching is successful, you can access members of the instance using the bound variable, that is, o. The following diagram compares the code changes of using instanceof and matches. As is evident, the matches operator takes off the ugly explicit casting from the code:

| obj instanceof Ocean | obj matches Ocean o |
|---|---|
| ((Ocean)obj).getBottles(); | o.getBottles(); |

Let's see whether type matching eases our code with multiple occurrences:

```
void dyingFish(Object obj) {
    if (obj matches Ocean o) {                   // check & bind
        System.out.println(o.getBottles());       // extract
    }
    else if (obj matches Sea sea) {               // test
        System.out.println(sea.getDeadFish());
    }
    else if (obj matches River riv) {             // test
        if (riv.getPlasticBags() > 100) {    // cast & destruct
            System.out.println("Say no to plastic bags. Fish are
```

```
                dying!");
        }
    }
}
class Ocean { .. }
class Sea { .. }
class River { .. }
```

The test pattern is not limited to the `if-else` statements. Let's see how it can be used with `switch` constructs.

# Using pattern matching with switch constructs

The `switch` statement seems to be one of the best constructs that can use pattern matching. At present, a `switch` construct can match primitive literal values (excluding `long`, `float`, and `double`), `String`, and enum constants.

If a `case` label can specify a pattern, the code in the preceding section (the one that uses multiple instances of object checking and value extraction) can be modified as follows:

```
void dyingFish(Object obj) {
    switch (obj) {
        case Ocean o:    System.out.println(o.getBottles());
                         break;
        case Sea sea:    System.out.println(sea.getDeadFish());
                         break;
        case River riv:  if (riv.getPlasticBags() > 100) {
                             System.out.println("Humans enjoy! Fish die!");
                         }
                         break;
    }
}
```

With pattern matching, the business logic takes the limelight. It also reduces the complexity of the syntax, which improves code readability. The preceding code is also optimizable because we are likely to dispatch in *O(1)* time.

 Under pattern matching, work is also being done on the deconstruction pattern (which is the opposite of instance construction).

# Summary

In this chapter, you covered how pattern matching would change your everyday code. Pattern matching introduces a new keyword, `matches`, to ease the checking, casting, and retrieval of values from instances.

This book took you through the latest Java versions—10, 11 and 12, and also Project Amber. Java has a strong development road map and it continues to excite the developers and enterprises with its existing features and new capabilities. With a new six-month release cadence, Java is advancing at a fast pace that we haven't witnessed earlier. As developers, you get to work with newer Java features and improvements, sooner than ever before.

I encourage all developers to check out the improvements and additions to new Java versions, as they are released. Also, don't miss to browse through projects such as Valhalla, Loom, Panama, and many other projects at Oracle's website. These projects will advance Java's capabilities such as light-weight threading, simpler access to foreign libraries, and newer language candidates such as value types and generic specialization. Stay tuned!

# Other Books You May Enjoy

If you enjoyed this book, you may be interested in these other books by Packt:

**Mastering Java 11 - Second Edition**
Dr. Edward Lavieri

ISBN: 9781789137613

- Write modular Java applications
- Migrate existing Java applications to modular ones
- Understand how the default G1 garbage collector works
- Leverage the possibilities provided by the newly introduced Java Shell
- Performance test your application effectively with the JVM harness
- Learn how Java supports the HTTP 2.0 standard
- Find out how to use the new Process API
- Explore the additional enhancements and features of Java 9, 10, and 11

**Mastering Microservices with Java - Third Edition**
Sourabh Sharma

ISBN: 9781789530728

- Use domain-driven designs to develop and implement microservices
- Understand how to implement microservices using Spring Boot
- Explore service orchestration and distributed transactions using the Sagas
- Discover interprocess communication using REpresentational State Transfer (REST) and events
- Gain knowledge of how to implement and design reactive microservices
- Deploy and test various microservices

# Leave a review - let other readers know what you think

Please share your thoughts on this book with others by leaving a review on the site that you bought it from. If you purchased the book from Amazon, please leave us an honest review on this book's Amazon page. This is vital so that other potential readers can see and use your unbiased opinion to make purchasing decisions, we can understand what our customers think about our products, and our authors can see your feedback on the title that they have worked with Packt to create. It will only take a few minutes of your time, but is valuable to other potential customers, our authors, and Packt. Thank you!

# Index

used, for accessing HTML pages 93, 95

# T

Thread Local Allocation Buffer (TLAB) 72
thread-local handshakes 57
time-based release versioning 61
TLS 1.3 130
traditional string literals
  concatenation, using 187, 188
  escape sequences, using 187
  used, for storing file paths 201
  versus raw string literals 192
traditional strings
  used, for writing database queries 201
traditional switch constructs
  issues 136, 137
transform() method 197, 198
Transport Layer Security (TLS) 121
type inference
  about 10
  in Java 25
  in Java 5 25
  in Java 7 26
  in Java 8 26
  using, with derived classes 17, 18
  using, with generics 21
  using, with interfaces 19
  using, with var 10, 11
  versus dynamic binding 31
  with var 68
type test patterns 216, 217
type testing
  issues 214, 215

# U

underscores
  used , for marking unused lambda parameters
  204
Unicode 10 128

Unicode language-tag extensions 58
Unicode Standard
  reference 128
unused lambda parameters
  marking, with underscores 204

# V

values
  reassigning, to inferred variables 23
var
  adding, to lambda parameters 68, 69
  challenges 27, 28, 29, 30
  lambda parameters, using 68
  type inference, using 10, 11, 68
  using, with arrays 20
  using, with primitive data types 15, 16
VM interface
  testing 79

# W

World Wide Web (WWW) 82

# X

XML data
  storing, as Java string 200

# Z

Z Garbage Collector (ZGC)
  about 101
  features 102
  tuning 108, 109
  working with 103, 104
ZGC heap 104, 106
ZGC phases
  about 106
  Pause Mark End 106
  Pause Mark Start 106
  Pause Relocate Start 106
ZPages 104